MANCHESTER CITY
GREATS

MANCHESTER CITY GREATS

IAN WHITTELL

Foreword by
FRANCIS LEE
Chairman,
Manchester City F.C.

SPORTSPRINT PUBLISHING
EDINBURGH

ISBN 0 85976 352 8

British Library Cataloguing in Pubication Data

A catalogue record for this book is available from the British Library

Typeset by ROM-Data Corporation,
Falmouth, Cornwall
Printed and bound in Great Britain by J.W. Arrowsmith Ltd;
Bristol

Foreword

It gives me great pleasure in this, Manchester City's Centenary year, to write the foreword to a book that recalls so many glorious moments in this great club's history.

I was privileged enough to have taken part in some of those successes and feel even more privileged to have become chairman of a club that still has some of the most intensely loyal supporters in the game.

It was you, the supporters, who wanted me to become involved in buying the club last year. Without your backing I doubt I would have done so.

Now the most important thing I can ask of you is to be patient, because together I firmly believe we can build something a bit special at Manchester City.

At the time of writing I have only been back at City for six months and, even though I believe we have taken great strides in that time, the problems that still exist here are amazing.

In those six months we have already spent nearly £4 million on phase one of Maine Road's re-development and by next March that figure will have risen to about £9 million.

This is part of a five-year plan that will turn Maine Road into a 45,000 all-seater ground and give the stadium and the club a complete face-lift.

Of course, what happens on the pitch is the most important thing at any football club and I believe that in my time here we have bought wisely and signed players who fit easily into the City tradition. We have a good squad with some real talent. Hopefully many of these players will one day be worthy of joining the long list of Manchester City Greats.

Francis Lee
Chairman
Manchester City

Acknowledgements

I am greatly indebted to a host of friends and colleagues for their assistance and support. In particular, the nine players I interviewed invariably gave their absolute co-operation. It was a pleasure to meet and talk to them all.

As one would expect of a club such as Manchester City, the staff with whom I came into contact were equally helpful. In particular, chairman Francis Lee and his close friends and fellow directors Colin Barlow and John Dunkerley co-operated in every way possible.

I am indebted to the *Newcastle Evening Chronicle* and *The Sun* newspapers for the loan of photographs, and to John Peters who helped collect a number of pictures. Dennis Tueart and Bobby Johnstone also proved invaluable with the loan of photos from personal collections.

Contents

Introduction

When Francis Lee launched a high-profile and ultimately success-ful campaign to become chairman of Manchester City in the autumn of 1993, the unexpected news should have been greeted with stunned amazement.

The fact that at Maine Road it was not, speaks volumes about one of English football's most unpredictable clubs. Any fan will tell you that supporting City, with their history of heroic successes and heartbreaking failures, may be frustrating but it is never dull or predictable.

Anywhere else, the news that one of a football club's most famous former players-turned-millionaire was about to try and buy out a regime that had been in power for two decades would have been something out of the ordinary. Not at City, a club that has given its followers the good and the bad, but rarely the ordinary.

When the Blues have been good – such as the side that Lee helped inspire in the late sixties – they have been glorious. When they have been bad, they have never done things by halves or given those fanatical followers an easy ride. Twice, for example, City have gone into the final day of a season needing a positive result to avoid relegation. Once, in 1959, they succeeded. Once, in 1983, they did not.

Where the club has never failed is in presenting the public with football talent worthy of attention. That is what makes the selection of just nine names from a list of great post-war players so daunting.

How, for example, can you omit Alan Oakes the man who played more games for the club than any other player in history? Or contemporaries like Mike Doyle, Glyn Pardoe and Neil Young who had so much to do with the glory years at Maine Road.

From the 1950s, how can you not mention Roy Clarke, Dave Ewing, Joe Hayes, Bill Leivers, Don Revie, Cliff Sear or Ken

Barnes who went on to serve the club brilliantly in coaching and scouting roles.

Denis Law, better known for his performances on the other side of Manchester, had a brilliant if brief City career. And from more recent years loyal servants like Tommy Booth, Willie Donachie, Dave Watson, Asa Hartford and Paul Power are worthy of honourable mentions.

The name of Rodney Marsh is still revered at Maine Road after providing fans with a tantalising glimpse of his exquisite skills. Unfortunately, he is also remembered for arriving at the club at the time they were in the process of losing the race for the 1972 title. In a similar vein, Trevor Francis looked like turning himself into a City legend just as the club decided to sell him.

In any case, the players featured in this book have undeniable claims to the title of City Greats. The Wembley Cup Final sides of the 1950s offer up brilliant keeper Bert Trautmann, inspirational larger-than-life skipper Roy Paul and superb inside-forward Bobby Johnstone. While only playing 124 games for City, the Scotsman made a lasting impression on all who saw him.

Three players from the 1960s are automatic choices and the names of Bell, Lee, Summerbee still roll off the tongue today. They are joined by their skipper Tony Book whose service behind the scenes with the club has lasted over quarter of a century and makes him the ultimate City man.

Giant goalkeeper Joe Corrigan overcame personal problems to play for England and win over City's loyal but demanding fans. He forms a convenient link between the glory days of the sixties and the next good City team of the mid 1970s, represented by that terrific winger Dennis Tueart. Tueart was a devastating player and the man whose unforgettable goal was responsible for City winning their last major trophy, the 1976 League Cup.

As chairman Francis Lee writes in his foreword to this book, the current City playing staff have a tremendous legacy to follow. But recent events at Maine Road suggest that if may not be long before there is a new generation of Manchester City Greats to be written about.

Ian Whittell
1994

CHAPTER ONE

Francis Lee

Bolton manager Bill Ridding got into his car outside Burnden Park and told Francis Lee, the Lancashire club's star forward, to follow him.

It was October 1967 and Lee, a 23-year-old of great promise, was in the middle of a bizarre one-man strike. Having served the terms of his contract with the second division club, he had effectively 'retired' from the game as a protest against Bolton's refusal to sell him.

Now, Wanderers had changed their stance, and Lee knew he was bound for one of two first division clubs for transfer talks. One was Stoke City, the other Manchester City.

'I jumped into my car and followed Bill down the new M62, it had opened just a couple of weeks earlier,' says Franny. 'I realised I was heading south and suddenly remembered I hardly had any petrol in the car.

'I remember thinking, I hope it's Manchester. If I had been going to Stoke, Bill would have arrived there on his own and I would have been stuck on the motorway somewhere!'

Fortunately for the petrol tank – not to mention City – Lee was indeed bound for Maine Road. The final piece in the jigsaw being assembled by Joe Mercer and Malcolm Allison. His arrival marked the start of a heady four-year period during which Manchester City would become one of the most talked-about and admired names in European football.

It also marked the start of a love affair between City fans and Lee that has endured over a quarter of a century and which reached an unforgettable peak at the start of the 1993–94 season when the former player, turned multi-millionaire businessman, launched a spectacular boardroom takeover.

City had slumped to the foot of the Premier League and

controversially replaced manager Peter Reid with the relatively unknown Brian Horton when Lee finally decided to end his self-imposed football exile and attempt to buy the club he once helped to such unforgettable success.

Backed by Colin Barlow, a talented winger for City in the pre-Lee sixties, and multi-millionaire businessman John Dunkerley, and buoyed by a phenomenal wave of public support, Franny set off on his mission.

It was a long and bitter battle as reigning chairman Peter Swales steadfastly refused to relinquish control. But as the season became increasingly desperate for the Blues, the sheer weight of public pressure mounted. Eventually, early in February 1994, Swales bowed to the inevitable and Francis Lee was City's new chairman.

'The biggest factor in my decision to become involved was, very simply, the fact that the people wanted me to get involved,' explains Lee. 'There were two or three people with money already in the club who wanted to put more in, as well as people outside the club who were interested in investing. And, of course, there were those fabulous fans who backed me every inch of the way.

'But the first thing we had to concentrate on was taking over and helping the club out of the terrible predicament they were in. That was my main motivation. Even though I had drifted away from football, I still held City dear and their lack of success over the years obviously disappointed me. It was, and is, a great club but there's no doubt in my mind that if we had not got involved at that point, City would have been relegated.

'With the financial state of the club at the time, if that had happened I believe it would have taken three years, and a large injection of cash, to get the club back into the Premiership. That would have been three wasted years for City and the fans.

'People liked to assume that this was a very personal, private war between Peter Swales and myself, that we were hurling spears and slinging rocks at each other. But the truth is that I have never had a wrong word with him and we still have a brief chat whenever we bump into each other.

'The simple fact is that a football club is no different to any other business. If the person running that business has not been successful the time comes when he has to be replaced. His track record for winning things was not good and I wanted to change that.'

First, Lee and his consortium had to convince Swales to walk away from a club he had ruled for the best part of 20 years. That did not prove an easy task and, as more legal and financial obstacles appeared, Lee became increasingly frustrated.

He recalls: 'The incumbents just did not want the change to happen and didn't believe it would happen. But eventually we realised that it had to happen for the club to stay in the Premier League. If I had been a hard-nosed businessman and not had the good of the club at heart I could have waited for City to go down and then bought the club for a song.

'But I would have been vilified for that and would have left the supporters with a three year wait before we could get the club up. Finally, we made a decision to go for broke and, thankfully, our offer was eventually accepted.

'That isn't to say I wasn't frustrated as the thing dragged on. I went on a family holiday to Barbados at Christmas and flew back in the middle of January, supposedly to complete the takeover. Of course there were yet more problems and that was the closest I came to throwing in the towel.

'I honestly thought we would never do it. I returned to Barbados, we exchanged a thousand faxes and finally came up with a formula that worked. In the meantime City were still in deep water and it was obvious the whole place needed turning round.

'We signed for the club and took over in February but I'm convinced that if we had been in charge a couple of months earlier the club would have been in a lot healthier state and the spirit would have been a lot better at Maine Road.'

With the injection of new capital came new players – Everton winger Peter Beagrie, Portsmouth striker Paul Walsh and German forward Uwe Rosler the most noteable – who helped City climb away from the relegation zone with something to spare.

The summer of 1994 brought bold new plans for ground re-development, a new face with an old name in England under-21 international Nicky Summerbee and, most important of all, renewed enthusiasm and optimism among City supporters.

The fact that Lee could spark such an instant change for the better at Maine Road should have come as no surprise to anyone who charted his meteoric City playing career. Lee had made just such an impact following his first arrival at Maine Road, 27 years earlier, when Allison and Mercer talked the young striker into completing a £60,000 transfer from Bolton.

In the 11 games before Lee's arrival at the start of that 1967–68 campaign City had suffered five defeats. They would suffer just five more over the rest of the season en route to capturing the League Championship for only the second time in the club's history.

Lee's debut, in a 2–0 home win over Wolves, marked the start of an 11-match unbeaten run, consisting of eight wins and 31 goals, eight of them from Lee himself.

'I'm not claiming any particular credit for the run, I just remember thinking that it was the longest unbeaten run I'd ever been involved in,' he says.

'After an unhappy end to my days with Bolton, it was a completely different atmosphere at City. As soon as you got into coaching sessions all they were interested in was attacking.

'I was used to Bolton's theory of building performances on defence, this was exactly the opposite; we had five great forwards and for a goalscorer such as me, it couldn't have been easier to slip into a side like that.'

City's excellent run came to a potentially disastrous end at Christmas 1967. Two meetings with West Brom in five days – and two defeats.

'We lost 3–2 at their place on Boxing Day,' says Lee, a City goalscorer that day. 'But even then, we murdered them!'

Albion inflicted City's second – and last – home defeat of the season five days later by a 2–0 scoreline to further question the Blue's Championship credentials. In spite of City setting off on another unbeaten run – this time lasting seven games – it wasn't until Lee and co. visited Old Trafford for a midweek fixture in late March that those questions would finally be answered.

'By Christmas I think we sensed we were going places,' says Lee. 'There was obvious disappointment over the West Brom games but the run after that really pushed us into the top bracket.

'And that United game really made people take notice. Everyone

Franny pictured on one of his 27 England appearances.

talks about "The Ballet on Ice", when we hammered Spurs at Maine Road in the December. But in terms of domination within Manchester itself, that was the game for me.

'We completely murdered them. George Best put them 1–0 up inside a minute, but we came back to walk it 3–1. To take over as number one in Manchester was very important, from our point of view as well as the fans. And with them challenging us near the top, it was an even more important result.

'In all my years at City, I played in 16 or 17 derby games, and only lost about three.'

Lee's memory plays tricks on him slightly. His record in League and cup derbies is even better! In 15 appearances against the old 'enemy', Lee ended on the winning side nine times, drawing four and losing just twice. In addition, he scored ten vital goals – including a penalty at Old Trafford in March '68 that helped City on their road to the Championship.

'We had known at Christmas that if we could dispel the defensive lapses that were caused by over-enthusiasm, we could beat anyone,' explains Francis. 'And that is exactly how things went.

'We won eight of our last 12 games, 13 of our last 18. When you are on a roll like that, there is not a lot your rivals can do.'

Lee's introduction to the City attack on the right wing undoubtedly helped lift the Blues above their rivals. Immediately after the West Brom reverses, City picked up invaluable 3–0 away wins at Nottingham Forest and Sheffield United. In the latter, Ken Mulhearn saved a penalty while Lee netted one at the other end. Before his arrival at Maine Road, City had struggled to find a consistent spot-kick taker; now they had one of the greatest.

There was an element of luck about the goal Lee netted against Arsenal to earn City a point, his miskicked volley spun into the goal while Tony Coleman distracted the keeper. But Lee scored winners in consecutive 1–0 victories over Sunderland and Burnley – the latter yet another spot kick.

By the penultimate weekend of the season, Leeds and Manchester United remained City's main rivals as the Blues headed for a tricky fixture at Tottenham. City need not have worried as a superbly emphatic 3–1 win set up one of the greatest ever Championship finales.

Leeds' defeat at home to Liverpool had left United as City's only rivals and while they hosted Sunderland on the final day of the season, City headed to the North-east and Newcastle's St James' Park. As Colin Bell, Mike Summerbee and Tony Book reminisce elsewhere in this book, it was a game no-one involved will ever forget.

'The whole of Manchester was geared to that weekend and to those games,' says Lee. 'And what a tremendous game ours was, probably one of the best I've ever played in, certainly in terms of excitement. There wasn't a bad goal among the seven. And there were some good ones disallowed as well.'

Fittingly, Lee was on the scoresheet in the 4–3 win that gave City the title by two points over United, beaten 2–1 by Sunderland. His contribution – a lethal finish from Bell's brilliant through ball – gave City a 4–2 cushion, an advantage they needed as the Geordies pulled a goal back with five minutes remaining.

City were Champions, Lee an England international, and the gamble he had taken eight years earlier fully vindicated.

Born and raised in Westhoughton, near Bolton, Lee had risen through representative schoolboy football, leaving school at 15 to become a draughtsman.

'I went to college in Horwich but left to sign for Bolton. The principal said I was stupid but my father, who had spent 40 years working in a cotton mill doing something he didn't like, said why not give it a crack.

'He said I could always go back to college if I didn't make the grade and the idea was to give myself 12 months. Within six months I thought I had a chance of making it.'

On November 5th, 1960, he was proved right. Aged 16, Lee's League debut – including a goal – came at Burnden Park in a 3–1 win. The opposition . . . Manchester City.

'I scored at exactly 3.15. I know because there was a photo of me the next day, heading the ball past Bert Trautmann with the time on the stand clock in the background.'

Lee's future City team-mate Denis Law scored the consolation goal and the youngster was off on a heady Bolton career that saw him lead Wanderers' scoring charts every season until his departure.

'It was enjoyable at Bolton, but frustrating,' he says. 'I really wanted to get away from the age of 18 or 19, because I could see they were going nowhere. The wages were poor and the club just wasn't changing with the times on or off the field.'

Lee had already scored double figures for Bolton by the time his dissatisfaction reached its peak in the autumn of '67.

'My contract was up in the June and they didn't want to sell me, so I signed a monthly contract,' recalls Lee. 'Bolton said they would never sell me and offered £150 a week to stay. I was only on £30 at the time, but I knew the only chance to further my ambition was to leave.

'By October I had served my contract, and the option, and virtually retired! I hadn't played football for about three weeks. I just did a bit of training on my own.

'Eventually, Bolton realised they had a rapidly depreciating asset. They could have got £60,000 plus a lad called Terry Wharton from Wolves a few weeks earlier. In the end, they got £60,000 from City, then spent all that money on Wharton. His value had doubled in a matter of days!

'Apart from City and Stoke, Liverpool were interested and Bill Shankly never tired of telling me in later years that not signing me was his biggest mistake. I used to dodge dear old Bill in the end, I got so tired of hearing that story!'

With Mike Summerbee coping admirably at centre-forward, Lee came into the City line-up on the right-wing. As they found the going tough in their Championship-defending season, Mercer and Allison made a switch that was to excite football fans around the world – Summerbee moved wide on the right and Lee took over the number nine shirt.

'Having murdered everybody in my first season, we floundered as soon as the next season started,' explains Lee. 'We thought we had a divine right to go out and thrash people. Mike didn't start very well at centre-forward because opponents got wise to his style. So they changed us.

'I was perfectly happy, it didn't matter where I played. But I don't think centre-forward was my best position. I was happiest when I was supporting a big striker.

'When I played for England, Geoff Hurst was the striker up front, and when City bought big Wyn Davies I scored 33 goals one season. In my time at Maine Road there was talk of buying Joe Royle or Bob Latchford or John Toshack and I think if we had, my record would have been even better.'

In '68–69, the compensation for League disappointment was considerable – an F.A. Cup winners' medal and, for Lee, the fulfilment of a promise he had made himself three years before that triumph in March 1969.

'I had been to the F.A. Cup Final between Everton and Sheffield Wednesday in 1966 and said to a pal: "I enjoyed that, but I'll never come here again unless I'm playing."

'I was delighted to beat Leicester and win the cup, but I didn't have the best preparation for the Final. I'd been out since the semi with a leg strain, and though I was fit for the Final, I had missed a couple of weeks training.

'I don't think I played outstandingly, I just had an average game which was a shame.'

The run to Wembley had provided some highlights, with City conceding just one goal in seven games, including the 1–0 Wembley triumph. City won four of their ties by 1–0 scorelines in some tense games. Apart from a nerve-testing semi-final victory over Everton, there had been a close quarter-final win by the same margin over Spurs at Maine Road.

'For me, that was the most important win,' says Lee. 'It was a tense and tight game; Spurs had come to defend and I got the winner towards the end. I played a 1–2 with Mike Summerbee and hit a half-volley into the net.

'I was struggling with the leg strain in the semi which was a disappointment, and the Final itself wasn't our greatest performance. The pitch was terribly bumpy and didn't do us any favours. On a true Wembley surface we would have annihilated Leicester.'

City's first foray into unknown European waters ended in disaster that season, an embarrassing first round exit at the hands of Turkish side Fenerbahce – 'Even with our legs tied, we should have won that,' says Lee, still disgusted by City's poor showing.

'Mind you, it was a dangerous atmosphere out there. I think if we had got over that hurdle we would have done alright. Malcolm Allison had added a bit of pressure by saying how well we would do in Europe, but he wasn't far wrong. After all, we won the Cup Winners' Cup the following season.'

And the League Cup. In 1969–70 City became the first English club to win a domestic and European trophy in the same season. The League Cup triumph was all the more rewarding for the Maine Road faithful including, as it did, a semi-final victory over Manchester United.

'The problem that season had been that we were making changes in defence and altering our style slightly,' says Lee. 'But we were still good enough to win cups.'

The two-legged semi-final with United was played in front of a combined crowd of nearly 120,000 and included one of the most bizarre derby goals ever in the crucial 2–2 second leg draw at Old Trafford.

'We had a free-kick outside their box near the end with United leading 2–1,' recalls Lee. 'I assumed it was direct and their keeper Alex Stepney did as well. I drove it in, Alex parried, and Mike Summerbee put the rebound in.

'Neither of us had noticed the ref had his arm up for an indirect free-kick! He had given obstruction instead of a foul. Obviously, if we had noticed, I wouldn't have had a shot and Alex wouldn't have gone near it.'

The decisive first leg had ended in a 2–1 City victory and more controversy. It included a late penalty winner from Lee – after a trip on him by Nobby Stiles – and furious disputes after the final whistle. An enraged George Best knocked the ball out of referee Jack Taylor's hands and was later fined and suspended.

A 2–1 Wembley win over West Brom completed the first part of the cup-double. A miserable Vienna evening against Gornik Zabrze a month later was the scene for part two. That European Cup Winners' Cup run included some of the most memorable nights in City history.

'For me, the best was probably the very first game, in Bilbao,' says Lee. 'They had a great team on paper and it was our first European match since the Fenerbahce games. You wouldn't fancy us to even score, yet we got three and came back with a good draw.'

Yet another Lee penalty – this time for a foul on Neil Young just before half-time – put City 2–0 up in the Cup Winners' Final. And even though the travelling Mancunians among the paltry 12,000 crowd had an anxious final 22 minutes after the Poles pulled a goal back, there was a great deal of merriment among the City contingent on the flight back to Britain.

Mike Summerbee recalls how Lee enlisted the help of a stewardess to pass a note to Mercer warning him that the stranger next to him was a suspected hijacker. 'Keep him talking,' said the note and Mercer tried to oblige – all the way from Austria to Manchester!

Lee's role at Maine Road was not limited to that of match winner. He was an integral part of the brilliant team spirit which pervaded the club during those successful seasons.

Along with his partner 'in crime' Mike Summerbee – who would later play a key public relations role in Lee's takeover battle – Franny can lay claim to a place among the most popular players ever to pull on a City shirt.

Says Lee: 'In those days, we would have pantos at the social club every Christmas and when we got back to the ground after away games we would pop our heads in at the social club for 20 minutes or so to say hello. If we'd done well, we might get on stage and give a song!'

Sadly, 1970–71 saw City off-tune, hampered by a lengthy injury list. Untried youngsters found it difficult to settle and there was board room unrest that dragged Mercer and Allison along.

'They got sucked into the arguments and things started to fall apart from then on,' says Lee. 'It was a difficult situation and one that was bound to have an unsettling effect.'

Nevertheless, Lee was set for the most successful goalscoring season of his life in '71–72. Supported by Wyn Davies, a £60,000 buy from Newcastle, he was at last able to play his favoured 'supporting role' alongside the big Welshman.

By March, City were first division pacesetters, along with Derby, Leeds and Liverpool. Lee, who would finish with an astonishing 33 League goals, including 13 penalties, felt the title was there for the taking. Malcolm Allison felt otherwise, master-minding a big money £200,000 move for the brilliant, if unpre-dictable, Rodney Marsh.

'At Easter we were odds on to win the League, but Rodney just wasn't the player for us at the time,' says Lee, confirming a popular theory. 'He disrupted our pattern. But, having said that, you can't blame Rodney for everything.

'We had some abysmal luck. I can think of about three blatant penalties we should have had. If the ball isn't running for you, you don't win Championships.'

A dismal run of three wins in the final eight games ensured that was precisely what happened. Coincidentally, Lee and Marsh were the scorers in a brilliant final game of the season when City beat Derby 2–0 in front of 55,000 at Maine Road.

But the Blues knew they could not win the title. Two of their rivals, Derby and Liverpool, had to meet after City had com-pleted their fixtures. Twelve days later, it was Derby who were crowned Champions – one point above fourth-placed City.

For all that disappointment, Lee had the consolation of his remarkable scoring record, and a well-deserved reputation as the best penalty taker in the game.

Goal poacher . . . Lee causing panic in another opposition defence.

'I had taken penalties from the age of 17 but I didn't particularly enjoy it,' he admits. 'It's a thankless task. What people tend to forget is that I only ever took two penalties for England – and I missed them both!

'One was in Portugal where the ground was so heavy my standing foot got caught and I mishit the ball so badly I wouldn't have hit two goals. And the other was when I hit the crossbar against Wales.'

To the uninitiated, Lee's penalty technique looked crudely effective – a long run up followed by an aimless blast.

'That's just not true,' says the man himself. 'Everyone said I blasted the ball, but I used to aim for the stanchion and hit the ball at three-quarter speed, pretending I was passing the ball 50 or 60 yards.

'I would take a long run-up to give the keeper longer to think about it, it gave him less of an idea which side I was going to hit it.

'And of course I practised a lot. I would tell our keeper in training which side I was going to shoot because if you could beat a first division goalie ten times out of ten when he knew where the ball was going, you would have no trouble in a game situation. Then, the only problem is the pressure, and I was able to stick that to the back of my mind.'

Along with the reputation as a great penalty taker came an unwanted tag – that of great penalty winner. The joke went that City had signed a new Chinese player, 'Lee Won Pen'. Franny raises a knowing grin before launching into a defence he must have made hundreds of times over the years.

'Of those 13 penalties in '72, I probably won about three,' he says. 'I always said if I had been awarded the number of penalties I deserved, you could add 100 goals to my career. I can't think of more than three or four dubious penalties I ever won, and I can tell you umpteen I should have got.

'In the end, this reputation undoubtedly worked against me. Once, playing for Derby against Wolves, I flicked the ball over this guy's head and he came through chest high, took my shirt off, tore my shorts and left a huge scar on my legs. And the ref said I dived!

'The season I got 13, I should have had a lot more. We had one shot palmed over against Arsenal and, against Ipswich, Mick Mills committed the most blatant handball I have EVER seen. Neither was given.'

The end of that term also saw Lee's England career draw to a close after 27 internationals – including just three defeats – and ten goals.

'My only regret is not leaving Bolton sooner,' he says. 'If I had, I think I could have played 50, maybe 70, times for England. I didn't make my debut until I was 24.

'I played three games in the 1970 World Cup Finals and I felt we had a better side than in '66. The players who had won the Cup were more experienced and I think the fringe players were better.

'If we hadn't gone out to West Germany in extra-time in the quarters, I think we would have gone on to win it. Brazil certainly didn't fancy playing us.'

That numbing 3–2 defeat by Germany was Lee's last involvement in a World Cup tie, although he was tempted to call manager Alf Ramsey three years later as England prepared for a crucial qualifying game with Poland.

'I hadn't played an international for over a year but I knew those Poles so well from European games with City. I thought I knew the best way of unlocking them.

'I very nearly rang Alf to ask him to pick me. I don't know what he would have said though. He'd probably have told me to get lost in no uncertain terms.'

On the home front, Lee again had cause to bemoan his luck with penalty decisions the following season as City – now without Mercer who had left for Coventry – struggled to reassert themselves. In a 0–0 draw at Highbury, everybody in the ground saw Arsenal's Jeff Blockley handle – everybody, that is, except for referee Gordon Hill who had been blinded by the sun.

'I got my revenge,' jokes Franny. 'The next time he refereed one of our games, I was waiting for him in the tunnel with a pair of sunglasses. "You'd better stick these on," I told him.'

Typically, Lee had some interesting encounters with officials during 1972–73. At White Hart Lane, his Diego Maradona impression earned City a 3–2 win against Spurs as he palmed the ball over the line.

'I dived to head the ball and it caught my hand. The ref was an obnoxious sort and, if he had asked me had I handled it, I would have told him yes. After the match, the press lads did ask me, and I had to admit that I had and I never expected the ref to give it.'

His most interesting brush with officialdom, however, came in a 1–1 draw at Sheffield United in December. 'I was sent-off, and it was all Mike Doyle's fault,' laughs Francis.

'He had two or three skirmishes with Trevor Hockey and the ref was handling it so badly that when the game stopped I told him, "I hope you don't read the papers because I've never seen a ref get less than five out of ten . . . and you will!"

'A bit later, Trevor made an innocuous tackle on me, we both fell down and the ref shouted "Get off you!" at me. All I'd been doing was trying to cheer him up, and that's how he repaid me!'

Away from the fun, there was an increasingly sad side to life at City. Mercer had left for Coventry in June '72, Allison left before the '73–74 season. Johnny Hart, Tony Book and Ron Saunders would all take the revolving door into the City manager's office during the coming season, Lee's last as a City player.

Says Lee: 'We got to the League Cup Final against Wolves, should have won it and didn't. Ron was in charge at the time and, quite simply, he couldn't handle the big-name players.

'One day he made Denis Law ballboy in shooting practice! That was the worst thing he could possibly have done. Ron was more a manager of good, middle-of-the-road pros, as he proved at other clubs.

'Having said that, when he was sacked there was all this talk of player power. But I went down to the dressing room as soon as I heard about the sacking and said to him, "If you got fired because of the way you treated me, you can rest assured I had nothing to do with it. I had no part whatsoever in what has happened." And that was the complete truth.'

By the end of that season, new manager Tony Book, Lee's former skipper, was building an exciting new team. The established players were gradually being replaced and Derby manager Dave Mackay, returning from a summer tour, shot up to Manchester from Heathrow as soon as he heard Lee was available for £100,000.

'I didn't want to leave, I felt I had a couple more good seasons in me but Tony said he thought it would be better if I and Mike Summerbee went. I said, "OK. But you might regret it!" '

Lee's words were prophetic. In his very first season at the Baseball Ground, he helped County to the League title. His crowning glory could well have been a scintillating goal he struck in Derby's vital 2–1 win at Maine Road in late December.

'I think City would have won the League that season if I had stayed,' he says frankly. 'And a scriptwriter couldn't have done a better job when I got that goal at Maine Road. It gave me a lot of pleasure and I proved my point.

'The season before I signed for Derby, they won four away games. Dave asked me to try and help improve that record and we won seven after I arrived, and won the League.'

After one more season at Derby – including another foray into the European Cup – Lee decided to retire. The growing demands from his business enterprises meant he was driving over 60,000 miles a year, on top of full-time football. Those business interests, a story in themselves, eventually made Lee a millionaire and led to his dramatic Maine Road return.

'I started in the waste paper business in 1966, it seemed like common sense to me,' he explains. 'Sport is littered with examples of people who earned a lot of money and blew it. From day one I vowed that when I finished my standard of living would not drop.'

Lee has certainly succeeded in that regard. In 1977 he bought a spectacular Cheshire property and started a second successful sporting career by training race horses. Former England team mate Kevin Keegan, now the manager of Newcastle United, and current City striker Niall Quinn are among the owners who keep horses in Lee's stable.

It seems that in horse racing – as in business, as in football – Francis Lee is a born winner. City fans can only hope that winning streak continues in the seasons to come.

Francis Lee
FULL INTERNATIONAL CAPS—27 (10 goals)
(England score given first)

1968: Bulgaria (Wembley) 1–1.
1969: France (Wembley) 5–0 GOAL, Northern Ireland (Belfast) 3–1 GOAL, Wales (Wembley) 2–1 GOAL, Scotland (Wembley) 4–1, Mexico (Mexico City) 0–0, Uruguay (Montevideo) 2–1 GOAL, Holland (Amsterdam) 1–0, Portugal (Wembley) 1–0.
1970: Holland (Wembley) 0–0, Belgium (Brussels) 3–1, Wales (Cardiff) 1–1 GOAL, Colombia (Bogota) 4–0, Ecuador (Quito) 2–0 GOAL, Romania (Guadalajara) 1–0, Brazil (Guadalajara) 0–1, West Germany (Leon) 2–3, East Germany (Wembley) 3–1 GOAL.

1971: Greece (Wembley) 3–0 GOAL, Malta (Wembley) 5–0 GOAL, Northern Ireland (Belfast) 1–0, Wales (Wembley) 0–0, Scotland (Wembley) 3–1, Switzerland (Basle) 3–2, Switzerland (Wembley) 1–1, Greece (Athens) 2–0. 1972: West Germany (Wembley) 1–3.

MANCHESTER CITY APPEARANCES

League: 248 + 1 sub, 112 goals. F.A. Cup: 24, 7 goals. League Cup: 26, 14 goals. Europe: 22, 10 goals. TOTAL: 320 + 1 sub, 143 goals.

CHAPTER TWO

Bert Trautmann

The story of goalkeeping great Bert Trautmann is one of the most incredible in the history of British football – a tale any self-respecting Hollywood scriptwriter would have been proud to create.

It is a story inexorably linked with the rise to power of Adolf Hitler, the Second World War and Trautmann's laudable efforts to win acceptance from a nation with which he had been at war for four years.

Add an often stormy and tragic personal life and several controversial episodes on and off the field, and it is easy to appreciate the fascination the German held for football fans throughout the world.

He was a player the great Russian Lev Yashin once described as the only truly world class keeper – along with himself! Experts as diverse as Jimmy Hill, Bobby Robson, Don Revie and Tommy Docherty agree he belongs among the world's greatest.

An excellent biography, by Alan Rowlands, was published in 1990, breathing new life into the Trautmann legend and paving the way for a film. More than 30 years since he last kept goal for City, that legend has one remarkable episode that stands out – the 1956 F.A. Cup Final with Birmingham City.

With City out to make amends for their Cup Final defeat at the hands of Newcastle 12 months earlier, it appeared nothing could deny Trautmann his part in a footballing fairytale. Already installed as the country's player-of-the-year, he was enjoying a fine game as City romped towards a 3–1 victory.

With 15 minutes left, Birmingham forward Peter Murphy raced through and, with characteristic bravery, Trautmann flung himself at his opponent's feet, suffering a sickening blow to his neck from Murphy's knee.

'It was only years later I could piece together what happened that day,' says Bert nearly 40 years on. 'I was recently watching a video of the game for the first time and you can see me coming out to intercept the ball. I was more or less in the air and neither me nor Murphy could stop.

'He tried to get over me, lifted his left leg clear but caught me in the neck with his right. It was completely accidental. After that, I was gone.'

In obvious distress, Trautmann took many minutes to compose himself while receiving treatment but, in spite of skipper Roy Paul's wish to replace him with Roy Little, Trautmann insisted on staying in goal.

'A year earlier I had injured my neck training for the '55 Final and was convinced I was going to miss that game,' he continues.

'A blind physiotherapist in Eastbourne helped get me fit and when I broke down in '56, our trainer thought it was the same muscle problem. I played subconsciously after that, everything was grey until the final minute when I could see clearly again.

'I made a couple more saves but don't remember anything until the final minute when Dave Ewing, our big centre-half excused himself for colliding into me. Of course, I had no idea what I had done. I was only aware of this pain – like an extreme toothache – in my neck.'

That intense pain was not helped by the congratulatory slaps on the back as the final whistle confirmed City's precious victory. With his neck twisted at a grotesque angle, Bert was helped from the field and to City's victory celebrations.

'On Sunday morning I was taken to St George's Hospital in Kensington where they took X-rays and told me it was nothing. But I could not move my head. If I wanted to turn, I had to move my whole body.

'Back in Manchester, I must have looked like death. We had the homecoming in Albert Square, which was packed, and I had to say a few words. The thing I remember most was Frank Swift slapping me with his big hands; it felt like I had been split right down the middle with an axe!'

In desperation, Trautmann visited an osteopath who diagnosed the keeper had 'five vertebrae out of place.'

Bert with the 1953 City team. The line-up (back row left to right) Ewing, Revie, Branagan, Trautmann, Hannaway, Paul. (front row) Anders, Hart, Williamson, Broadis, Cunliffe.

Recalls Bert: 'I had no reason to disbelieve him, so he took my head and started turning it. The pain was crucifying, but he said he had managed to get four back in place.

'He then put my head on its side and hit me with the flat of his hand! Again, the pain shot through my middle. He told me to make another appointment, but I knew I would never be going back to him.'

It was only on a visit to medical friends at Manchester Royal Infirmary on the Tuesday that a horrified doctor informed Trautmann he had played the last 15 minutes of the F.A. Cup Final with a broken neck. The rough treatment handed out by the osteopath a day earlier could quite easily have killed the footballer.

There followed a complex operation, which involved holes being drilled into Bert's skull to accommodate a neck brace. The get well letters poured in as doctors said it would be at least a year before he could even consider playing football. But the goalkeeper had no doubts.

'I was in my early thirties, but I never really thought of the injury as being that serious,' he explains. 'There was nothing I could do but lie there and do a lot of thinking. And never did I think that I would not play football again.'

In true Hollywood tradition, the show would go on. Bernhard Carl Trautmann, then 32, would play again, and many more eventful episodes would be added to a story that began in the north German port of Bremen in October 1923. He was born into a country in the midst of great economic and political turmoil. Trautmann, a strong and athletic youngster, followed the example of the vast majority of his contemporaries, first joining the Nazi party's Jungvolk and later progressing to the Hitler Youth.

When Trautmann left school to become an apprentice with a diesel manufacturer in March 1939, World War II was only months away. Two years later, Bert decided to join the air force as a wireless operator, rather than wait to be conscripted.

A month later, he transferred to a parachute regiment and in later years would utter a claim surely unique among goalkeepers: 'I attribute my knack of cushioning the ball to my training as a parachutist,' said Bert. 'I was taught to brace my body against the shock of the landing.'

Trautmann would serve nearly three horrific years on the brutal Russian Front. Transferred to France in May 1944, he was taken prisoner on the Belgian-Dutch border early the following year, an incident that was to alter his entire life.

A succession of prison camps eventually led the 21-year-old to Ashton-in-Makerfield in Lancashire. The Germans were kept interned in the months following the war and the goodlooking and popular Trautmann – christened 'Bert' by local girls – eventually decided his future lay in England.

His performances for the camp's football side had not gone unnoticed and, in August 1948, he made his debut for nonleague club St Helens Town. Nor had Trautmann gone unnoticed by Margaret Friar, the daughter of club secretary Jack. Within two years the couple would be married.

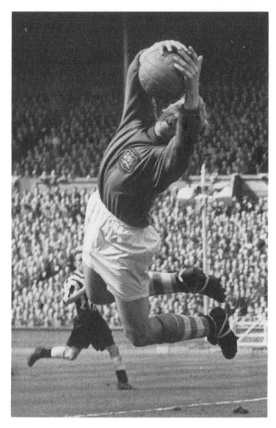

The greatest . . . Bert showing his ability in the '55 Cup Final.

Events continued at remarkable pace for Trautmann who, by October 1949, was attracting the attention of a number of professional clubs. Leading the chase for the German – still technically an 'alien' – were Burnley and Manchester City, looking for a replacement for the great Frank Swift.

Maine Road manager Jock Thompson and director Walter Smith were desperate to conduct talks with the utmost secrecy. Eventually they talked Trautmann into signing for them while he lay ill in bed, suffering from a bad bout of flu. Burnley were furious to find they had missed out on the budding star while sections of the public were staggered and outraged that City would sign a former German soldier.

Threatened by fan boycotts, City officials tried to temper the inevitable storm. Chairman Bob Smith issued a statement: 'One can understand the feeling of those who have suffered from the war, but we have to get down to the task of building a stronger team.'

In Trautmann's carefully stage-managed arrival at Maine Road, captain Eric Westwood added: 'There's no war in the dressing room and you're as welcome as any other member of the staff.'

The new keeper made his first City appearance in a 1–0 reserve defeat at Barnsley, but that and a further four reserve outings could not prepare him for the response that met his first team debut on November 19 at Bolton. The effect of the taunts from the crowd were not made any more bearable by the fact the self-critical keeper was on the receiving end of a 3–0 defeat.

'I was obviously nervous before the game,' says Bert. 'But Frank Swift came in and give me a piece of advice I always remembered. He said: "Son, there are nearly 40,000 spectators out there. Don't worry about them; ignore them."

'I completely shut the crowd out of my mind, something I did throughout my career and which some people thought was arrogant. I had quite a good first half, although we conceded a penalty in the second – the first goal I ever conceded in the Football League was a penalty.'

The feared boycott did not materialise in a 4–0 home debut win over Birmingham as Bert continued to obliterate the controversy from his thoughts. He recalls: 'I had no doubt in my mind I could make it as a professional and my confidence grew with each game. But I knew there was quite a lot of animosity about my signing.'

His confidence could not have been boosted by the 7–0 hammering Derby handed him in his next outing. 'I felt so bad about that,' he says. 'And I always looked forward to going back to Derby in later years to try and show I wasn't that bad a keeper. The pitch was ankle deep in mud that day. I went out, stood half a yard off my line and couldn't move for 90 minutes!'

Such results would lead to relegation for the Blues. Even so, Bert put in one particularly inspired display at Fulham – on his first game in London – and the crowd response suggested the worst days of his persecution were behind him.

'I had been getting a good press in the North-west, but my father-in-law pointed out that my first game in London would really test my mettle because of the papers and publicity down there.

The fateful moment . . . Trautmann bravely hurls himself at the feet of Birmingham's Peter Murphy. A split second later, his neck is broken.

'The papers said we should have lost by nine or ten that day, but we only lost 1–0. In the context of the early days, it was the best game I ever had – an experience you cannot describe – and the game that had the biggest influence on my career.

'I was at the Thames End of the ground and was the last player to come off. Both teams stood at the dressing room entrance and applauded; a very emotional moment. I was lucky in later years to win the Cup, win the player-of-the-year and play for the Football League. But Fulham was my greatest moment.

'I also particularly remember a 2–1 win at Sunderland for three reasons. It was our first and only away win of the season, in mid-April. It was also our first "double" over a team. And I saved two penalties!

'I saved one from Jack Stelling, the Sunderland rightback, but the ref said I moved. So he took it again, and I saved it again. Dennis Westcott went up to the ref and asked him which save he thought was better!'

Thompson's resignation led to the arrival of Les McDowall as manager; his first act was to sign two players who would prove inspirational figures in later seasons – defender Roy Paul and wing-half Ken Barnes.

For his part, still an 'alien', Bert was forced to work part-time as a mechanic while his earnings as a footballer amounted to £5 a week. That didn't stop him becoming a popular and important figure in the Maine Road dressing room.

A second place finish returned City to the first division and, by the start of the '51–52 season, things were looking ever brighter for 'Trauty', wife Margaret and son John. His 'alien' status was removed in 1952, enabling him to sign a new contract at £12 a week as City spent heavily on Don Revie and Ivor Broadis. Yet the expected success did not materialise.

Trautmann was under constant pressure. City hit an awful run in the New Year, crowds were down to 14,000 and the club only just held onto their first division status. It is still hard to know why City went so far wrong.

'We were never a great side in spite of having some real quality players like Revie, Johnstone, Clarke. We just didn't have quality in depth,' he notes.

Amid these disappointments, Trautmann, now re-united with his family and a celebrity in his homeland, was considering a return to the Continent.

An unsavoury incident played itself out during 1952 with Schalke 04 and Cologne desperate to sign Bert, both making illegal contact to offer huge salaries and the incentive of a place in Germany's impressive national squad.

City demanded a colossal £20,000 for the player, the Germans could not meet such a sum and, by December, the storm had played itself out. It was still the same depressing story at Maine Road, however, with City avoiding relegation by the slenderest of margins. The following season, '53–54, arrived with Trautmann privately hoping it would be his last at Maine Road.

After impressive pre-season performances with City in Germany had enhanced Trautmann's standing in his homeland, little happened in the coming season to alter his hope. With McDowall's eccentric tactics and a long injury list, City eventually finished 20th.

By the time he returned to West Germany on another preseason tour in 1954, his faith in City's future was only kept intact by the fledgling success of the Revie Plan.

McDowall returned from that German trip with his head full of Continental-inspired ideas. With Trautmann's distribution and brilliant throwing an integral part of the scheme, City used the Revie Plan in their first team for the first time in '54–55.

'We used it in our first game and lost 5–0 at Preston,' recalls Trautmann. 'Everyone jeered and laughed but McDowall told us we were going to persevere and eventually we proved we had the players to make the system work.'

Ken Barnes, an excellent attacking wing-half, was an important addition for the next game as City hammered Sheffield United 5–2 and the plan was a success . . . of sorts.

By the time the heavier pitches of late Autumn came into play, the plan floundered slightly. In a dreadful 5–1 home defeat by Charlton in November, Trautmann's short temper flared up over a disputed penalty. The keeper petulantly made no effort to save the kick and he and Roy Paul were involved in an altercation with the referee after the game that resulted in a fine and suspension for Bert.

Nevertheless, the Revie Plan came into its own in the one-off situations of the F.A. Cup. By the time Roy Clarke's winner beat Sunderland in the semi-final in late March, the double was a distinct possibility.

Unfortunately, minds were very much on Wembley as City's League form dipped and the Blues had to settle for seventh place. That Wembley date took on added importance.

City's build-up was hampered by a long injury list that included the keeper himself, but the blind physiotherapist ensured Trautmann fulfilled his dream.

'In 1954, West Germany won the World Cup and the following November they came over to play England at Wembley,' says Trautmann. 'I was the official interpreter and went to the stadium on the day before the game. I stood under the goal and said "Wouldn't it be marvellous to play here just once." Six months later, I was there.

'Today, I don't think the occasion means that much anymore in terms of the community spirit and everyone singing "Abide with Me" and so on. When I went there, I enjoyed the whole thing, the build-up, the media attention, everything. I have never known nerves like I had that day; even when we went back a year later, they were still bad.'

Newcastle, however, would ruin Trautmann and City's big day, after the great Jackie Milburn headed the Geordies in front inside a minute.

'Look at the picture,' says the keeper. 'Jackie's head is dug right into his shoulders! Dear old Jackie never scored a header in his life.'

City would not recover from that start and the loss, through injury, of classy full-back Jimmy Meadows after only 20 minutes. Ever the perfectionist, Trautmann was not happy with the goals he conceded in the 3–1 defeat – particularly United's second, scored by Bobby Mitchell.

'I had made a couple of good saves, but I was probably at fault when Mitchell beat me at the near post. As a keeper, you show the striker that post and dare him to have a go, and he did just that.'

The consolation for the 31-year-old German was the fact he had a higher public profile than ever, and the events of 1955–56 would send that profile soaring. City embarked upon a season that, while typically inconsistent in parts, saw them finish fourth, their highest position since winning the League 19 years earlier.

But it was to be in the F.A. Cup that McDowall's side finally fulfilled its potential. Yet, as Bobby Johnstone recalls elsewhere in this book, City's return path to Wembley was far from smooth.

It was Trautmann who inspired City to the narrowest of wins in a fourth round tie at lowly Southend. The Roots Hall ground was ruined by rain, and the groundstaff's brainwave of soaking up water by laying sea shells on the surface! It didn't prevent Trautmann having one of the greatest games of even his remarkable career.

'Besides the strength and ability of your team, there is so much luck involved in winning the cup,' he explains. 'That's why winning the League is the harder and greater achievement.

'People say that game at Southend was my greatest and it was certainly memorable. There were bricks in the pitch and planks across all the mud and we were very lucky to win 1–0.'

The good fortune extended to Southend having a certain penalty turned down. City skipper Roy Paul conceded that fact to an

Safe hands . . . the best in the business denies Newcastle's great centre forward Jackie Milburn in the '55 Final.

opponent after the game. 'Don't worry,' deadpanned the Southend player. 'Trautmann would have saved it!'

For the second successive season, City would reach Wembley by a 1–0 scoreline, via a semi-final win over Spurs, and another huge slice of luck. Trautmann appeared to have given away a definite penalty, felling Tottenham's George Robb in the closing minutes. Incredibly, the referee waved play on.

Says Bert: 'I had to dive into a melee of players to try and grab the ball and just as Robb was ready to have a shot, I tapped his ankle. Which goalkeeper wouldn't have done the same? You didn't have to be Bert Trautmann to do that!

'The following week we had to go to Tottenham in the League, and the night before the match we all went to the cinema. There was a news reel on and it showed me bringing George down.

'I was sliding deeper into my seat and the whole cinema audience were booing me. I said to the lads that if they had known I was in there, I would have got lynched!

'The next day I had a good game, though we lost 2–1. But whatever saves I pulled off, I was booed non-stop.'

The agony . . . a poleaxed Trautmann is given emergency treatment while anxious players from both sides look on. Bobby Johnstone (number 7) cannot bear to look.

Trautmann had created his own date with destiny with that one desperate act in the semi-final. The hate mail, still continuing on a small scale, increased greatly after the Spurs game. As Bert recovered from his broken neck in the long months after Wembley, he had greater tragedy to contend with.

His young son John was killed in a road traffic accident three weeks after the Final, a crisis that would contribute to the eventual failure of Bert's first marriage. And Trautmann soon found himself in the midst of a crisis in his football career.

Only six months after breaking his neck, Trautmann was out of plaster. By early December, to his doctor's displeasure, he insisted on making a reserve comeback.

McDowall, under pressure from the success of the burgeoning young 'Busby Babes' at Manchester United eventually put his star back into the first team against Wolves on December 15 – only 224 days after the keeper's near fatal injury.

'It was very difficult coming back and I had some very indifferent games,' says Bert. 'I came back too quickly really. I would stand there with the forwards coming at me, saying "Come on, have a go, let me show you I'm still good." But it never happened like that.

'Off the field, the directors were giving the players ultimatums which didn't help and eventually I reckoned I was finished. I told Les McDowall this, but he told me not to be silly. I told him I had cost City at least six points, but Les just said: "Think of the number of points you've saved us over the years."

'It took me 18 months to be able to say "I'm back." Part of the problem was that I didn't have proper physio and massage on my neck after the operation. That's why my neck is still painful and restricted today, especially in cold weather.'

By the start of 1957–58, the City cup-winning side was breaking up and it was a surprise, to Trautmann as much as anyone, that the club managed to finish fifth – albeit after notching up the bizarre goal difference of 104–100!

Amazingly, Bert looks back and claims: 'That was probably my most enjoyable season! It was like the old joke "defences on top." It just goes to show, as well, that the best keeper is not automatically the one who lets in fewest goals.'

Trautmann was back to his old inspired self in '58–59, yet McDowall's eccentric tactics were more disastrous than ever. It was only in a nerve-testing final game of the season that City secured safety with a 3–1 win over Leicester and condemned Aston Villa – playing the same night at West Brom – to the second division.

Yet again, Trautmann, now nearly 36, considered retiring to concentrate on his future. However, two things prevented him taking that step – with his fitness, he believed himself capable of playing another four years at that level. As for his future, Trautmann felt secure, having been told he would have a job at the club after retiring.

The arrival of a brilliant young striker called Denis Law late in '59–60 made sure City again won the by-now familiar fight against relegation. And Law's one full City season, 1960–61, helped the team finish 13th.

For Trautmann, there was also the kudos of captaining an English League XI against the Irish League that season. Says Bert: 'I really felt so proud when I led the team out. I was the only player who was not an international, but we eventually overcame the Irish resilience and won 5–2. I suppose I should have been a

Up for the cup . . . Bert, in his days as Stockport general manager, counting tickets for a big F.A. Cup clash with Liverpool in 1965.

happy man, but I could not help thinking about what I had missed by not playing in international football.

'For me, the greatest thing was to play in the English League, but not playing for Germany was a disappointment. I had plenty of talks with Sepp Herberger, the manager, about it, but I think he was afraid to bring someone in from abroad.'

Trautmann was brilliant that term, his most stunning display coming in a 1–1 draw at White Hart Lane in mid-October as City became the first side to avoid defeat against champions-to-be Tottenham.

Bert and Law helped City stay up again, but the keeper was involved in unsavoury on-the-field fights against Cardiff and Wolves. His mood wasn't helped as Law left for Italy that close season and he was offered a paltry pay rise, in spite of the abolition of the maximum wage.

Says Bert: 'I thought I was still the best player at the club, even at my age, but they would only offer me £30 a week. New blokes were signing for £80 or £90 and that annoyed me, having been there for so long.

'When George Poyser eventually took over from McDowall, he had no idea about the game. I think the club acted stupidly and eventually I told them to put my understudy Harry Dowd in goal. I had had enough.

'Another thing that upset me was that I had always been told not to worry about the future, that I always had a job at City. But after my last game for the club in '64, I had to apply for work in writing, and then they turned me down.

'But I'm not bitter. I'm still tremendously fond of the club and wherever I lived throughout the world, I always kept in touch with their results on World Service. Now, I have a satellite dish, it's even better.'

After a 12th place finish in 1961–62, an offer of £35 a week somehow managed to convince the veteran keeper to play another season. It was a decision he would regret. Along with Neil Leivers and Joe Hayes, he was the only survivor from the relatively carefree days of the 1950s. A pessimistic pre-season gave way to a catastrophic opening day – an 8–1 defeat at Wolves.

Things scarcely improved and Trautmann's understandable frustration spilled over in a shocking 6–1 home defeat by West Ham in mid-September.

Bert, disputing the fifth goal, picked up the ball and raced towards the referee: 'The guy was at least five yards offside and I was really furious, I felt like exploding.

'I took the ball and made a drop kick at the ref from 30 yards. I bet if you did that 1,000 times, you wouldn't hit him cleanly once, but the ball hit him right between the shoulders and knocked him down.

'He wasn't to know it was deliberate though. It could have been accidental and I don't think he had the right to send me off! Anyway, the fans hadn't seen him point to the dressing room and assumed I was walking off in disgust at my teammates. I got a standing ovation!'

It also earned the fiery keeper a £10 fine, £35 in lost pay and a seven-day suspension and ensured Dowd would take his first team place on a permanent basis.

Relegation was inevitable, as was McDowall's resignation at the end of the season after 13 years in charge. The board appointed assistant Poyser as his successor, but his relationship with Trautmann was strained from the first meeting when he told the German he had never rated him!

This would finally be Trautmann's last season. Sadly, 1963–64 saw him play only three first team and eight reserve games. The last senior outing came on Good Friday 1964 in a 5–0 romp over Norwich at Maine Road. A clean sheet was the only fitting way for this most exceptional of goalkeepers to go out. But the Manchester public wanted to give their hero a send-off to really remember.

April 15 saw nearly 48,000 pack into Maine Road to watch a star-studded Manchester XI beat an International XI 5–4. It earned their hero £9,000 and the eloquent Trautmann made an address after the game that summed up the rapport he had with the City public.

'I have had some great moments in my life,' he said. 'I have had the honour of playing with some great players. I have had the honour of living among some of the best people in the world.

'Tonight I am very grateful and very humble. Not only for myself but on behalf of my family and the German people. I hope in some small way I have contributed something to make the world a nicer place to live in, God bless you all.'

Trautmann had a brief spell with non-league Wellington in Shropshire before helping improve the fortunes of nearby Stockport County as general manager.

Predictably, the Trautmann story after Maine Road is every bit as incident-packed as his football career. After unsuccessful coaching spells in Germany, Bert took his football talents to the far corners of the world, working as part of the German government's football development programmes.

His travels took in Burma, Tanzania, Liberia, Pakistan and Malta. They also took him through another marriage before he finally settled down to retirement in Rudesheim-am-Rhein with third wife Marlys in 1988.

It is with genuine modesty and understatement the German can say: 'City was a marvellous experience for me and I'm quite proud of what I did. The story itself is magnificent, I don't think there's another like it.'

There was also to be a sentimental farewell to Maine Road, as the special guest at a testimonial for former teammate, Johnny Hart, in 1974. To a remarkable reception, Trautmann kept goal for one half while a promising City keeper called Joe Corrigan kept for the other.

The fact Hart had insisted on Bert's presence spoke volumes for the man – as did the fact Corrigan spent his free half watching Trautmann from behind the goal.

After all, the most meaningful praise a professional sportsman can earn comes from his colleagues and adversaries. His friend Ken Barnes echoes the sentiments of a generation of footballers and supporters.

'I saw Frank Swift play and people always talk about him, Bert Williams, Gordon Banks, Peter Shilton, whoever. Quite honestly if there has ever been anyone better than Trauty, I would like to have seen him. Simple as that.'

Bert Trautmann
MANCHESTER CITY APPEARANCES

League: 508. F.A. Cup: 33. League Cup: 4. TOTAL: 545.

CHAPTER THREE

Roy Paul

Roy Paul, Manchester City's uncompromising Welsh half-back mounted the steps to the Wembley Royal Box for the second time in 12 months. A year earlier the City skipper had made the journey as losing F.A. Cup Final captain after his team's 3–1 defeat at the hands of a rampant Newcastle United. Now, he was about to enjoy his finest footballing hour.

Paul, at the age of 36, had just helped his gifted team demolish Birmingham City and a rash promise he had made in the wake of the Newcastle defeat had come to fruition.

Taking a leaf out of Sam Cowan's book 20 years earlier, the City skipper had guaranteed that the Blues would return to the Twin Towers to avenge their 1955 loss.

Thanks to goals from Bobby Johnstone, Joe Hayes and Jack Dyson, Paul had kept his vow.

'Before the Newcastle game, I had promised all the kids back in the Valleys that if we won the Cup I would take it home and go around the schools with it,' recalls Roy. 'To my disappointment we lost, which is when I made my prediction.

'Sam Cowan had been City skipper in 1933 when they lost the Cup Final to Everton 3–0. Afterwards, King George V told him hard luck, but Sam replied: "It's alright, we'll be back next year. I hope you can make it as well!"

'City got back and beat Portsmouth 2–1, so I could hardly go wrong by following his example could I?

'I suppose the prediction could have backfired and made me look a bit stupid, but all I could think about were the kids back home.'

Paul's Welsh international team-mate Noel Kinsey made the City skipper work for his winners' medal. He fired Birmingham's equaliser in the 14th minute, cancelling out Johnstone's opener.

'I was marking Kinsey and, at half-time, we were walking off when he turned to me and said: "We'll murder you in the second half."

'I said: "No. We'll murder YOU." And I'm glad to say that's exactly what happened. I hope I don't sound conceited, but even though Kinsey scored, I thought I had a blinder that day! We got two lovely goals in the second half and I collected the cup. A marvellous feeling, really out of the ordinary.'

And, just as important to the fiercely proud Welshman, he was able to fulfil his promise and take the trophy back to his native Valleys.

'The council hired a car for me to take around the schools and told me whatever petrol expenses I incurred, they would reimburse me. Do you know, I'm still waiting for the money!

'Anyway, I got a tremendous reception at the schools in the valleys and ended up going for a drink. I came home, parked the car outside my house and went straight to bed.

'The next morning, to my amazement, I found I had left the car windows open, with the F.A. Cup lying on the back seat! Anyone could have walked by and pinched it. The F.A. still don't know how close they were to losing the cup!'

Back in the Rhondda Valley today, enjoying his retirement, Paul can reflect on a career that lost its potentially greatest years to the Second World War.

By the time he signed for Manchester City in 1950 for the considerable sum of £25,000, Paul was already 30-years-old. Like Tony Book over 15 years later, the Welshman would lead City to great successes in the twilight of his career.

Paul lost six years in his twenties to National Service and says: 'The war definitely cost me some of the best years of my career.

'My nephew is Alan Curtis, who used to play for Swansea and Wales. He doesn't let me forget that he has won two more caps than me.

'But I point out that Wales only played three or four games a season in my day and that I lost those six seasons. But for that, I would have won a lot more than 33 caps.'

Called up at the age of 20 in 1940, Paul was posted to Devon where he guested for Exeter City in wartime games. Following a particularly impressive performance in a 3–1 win over Arsenal, after Monday morning parade, he was ordered to report to the commanding officer.

Royal welcome . . . Paul introducing the Duke of Edinburgh to Bobby Johnstone before the '55 Cup Final. Pictured (left to right) are Spurdle, Barnes, Johnstone, Hayes, Fagan and Ewing.

'I wondered what I had done wrong, but the Colonel said he had been at the game and congratulated me on my performance!' recalls Roy.

'He arranged for me to go on a physical training course and I spent the rest of the war as a sergeant PTI. I had it very easy, I used to referee football matches and blow the whistle four times – once to start the game, once for half-time, once for the re-start and once for the final whistle!

'And with my money from football, I felt like a millionaire. I was getting half a crown in the army, but Exeter paid me 30 bob a game, plus £1 for travelling and £1 for a meal.'

Paul was already a professional footballer by the time war started in 1939, having signed for Swansea City in 1937, aged 16, after being spotted playing for Ton Boys Club.

The move 'rescued' the youngster from his life as a collier and Paul made his second division debut just before the outbreak of war in 1939. Then Paul, like every other pro footballer, found his contract torn up.

After his six years of PTI, Paul returned to Swansea where his career almost took an unlikely turn. British stars like Charlie Mitten and Neil Franklin were leading an exodus to Colombia where huge money was on offer. That offer soon extended to Paul.

He explains: 'A scout for a club in Bogota, called Millionairos, asked myself and Jack Hedley from Everton over for trials. We went, and the Colombians offered me £3,000 to sign on there and then. But I turned it down. To be honest, I just didn't fancy it, mainly because of the language problems.'

Swansea were not impressed by Paul's trip to the other side of the world, and the Welsh international found himself on the transfer list. A number of English clubs, including Manchester United, were interested, but City came in with the firm offer.

'City had just been relegated, but Les McDowall told me about the set-up and I liked the sound of it,' says Paul.

The path was clear for Paul, appointed captain by McDowall, to make his debut in an attractive Maine Road clash with Preston, the opening game of the 1950–51 season.

'Preston were the better side that day – they ended up as second division champions that season – but we won 4–2,' recalls Paul.

'George Smith scored a couple for us, and I had my hands full with Tom Finney. For me, Finney was a tougher player than even Stanley Matthews.

'Matthews didn't like to be hit but Tom would take it and dish it back. Eventually, Tom got the ball and I really clobbered him; but he was a great sportsman as well as a great player. At the end of the match, he shook my hand and wished me all the best.'

City were going to need those good wishes before securing promotion as runners-up behind Finney's Preston. Although unbeaten in the first ten games of the season, the manner in which that run came to an end provided a taste of things to come. Leading Doncaster Rovers 3–0 at half-time, thanks to a George Smith hat-trick, City let the Yorkshire side come back to win the game 4–3!

'I also remember us leading Grimsby 3–0, but drawing 4–4 in the end,' says Roy. 'The manager played hell with us, but I think it was just a case of being over-confident.'

The early days . . . Roy (back row far left) with the City team in 1951. The line-up (back left to right): Paul, Rigby, Trautmann, Branagan, McCourt, Hannaway. (front row) Meadows, Revie, Westcott, Broadis, Clarke.

Much of that confidence spread from skipper Paul. A physical player ideally suited to 1950's football, Paul's commitment was unquestionable, his tactics sometimes borderline.

'I wouldn't say I was dirty,' he argues. 'Aggressive is the word I would use. I was fairly physical; at 5ft 10in and 13st I was quite a powerful machine; and dynamite in the air!

'I had been playing right-half for Swansea but Les McDowall moved me to the left which actually suited me better as a right-footed player.

'I enjoyed that first season with City and it was a magnificent feeling to get into the first division for the first time.

'The only thing I didn't like about Les was that he would never praise you, no matter how well you played. You could tell from his expression that he was satisfied, but he would never say anything. Mind you, if you had a bad game, he was quick to remind you!'

A bad run of only one win in six games just before Christmas rocked City although they stormed back with a 5–3 win over Sheffield United in early December.

41

'The lads were terrific that day,' says Roy. 'Jim Gunning and Ken Branagan made their debuts and Dennis Westcott scored a terrific goal.'

Westcott and Paul had a big part to play in a crucial Christmas Day win over Birmingham at Maine Road, the 3–1 victory coming courtesy of a goal by Westcott and two Paul penalties.

Explains Roy: 'I wasn't a particularly good penalty taker, I just hit them and hoped. Against Birmingham, the second hit the upright and bounced down behind the keeper.

'I missed a couple of penalties early the next season. The only reason I took them was because no-one else fancied it. I was glad when we finally bought Don Revie. Now, he was a proper penalty taker.'

Another bad run in March '51 again hampered City, but they bounced back in style, annihilating Barnsley 6–0 in front of nearly 43,000. 'They were embarrassing that day,' says Paul. 'They had a great half-back playing for them in Danny Blanchflower, but he had a bad afternoon as you can imagine.'

A point from a goalless draw at Sheffield United meant only Cardiff had a mathematical chance of catching City. Paul helped ensure his fellow Welshmen had no opportunity to pip City – draws against Notts County and Grimsby securing runners-up spot behind Preston.

Paul's first taste of football in the top flight was marked by typical inconsistency by City. A run of only two wins in the opening ten matches was arrested by the signings of Sunderland's Ivor Broadis and Revie from Hull.

'Don was a very good footballer,' says Roy. 'A nice person and a fine footballer. For a six-footer he couldn't head a ball and his left foot was a "swinger", but he could really use his right. The only problem was that it meant more work for Ken Barnes and myself at half-back.

'Ivor was a bit too lazy for my liking, but they helped us win a few games and made sure there was no danger of going down.'

That was in spite of a three-month patch between January and April without a single win. Not surprisingly, a crowd of only 13,842 – at the time the lowest in Maine Road history – saw a home defeat by West Brom in early April.

A kiss for the cup . . . Paul lifts the 1956 F.A. Cup.

For the City skipper, there was the consolation of being able to relinquish penalty duties after a hectic September. He scored a last minute spot kick to rescue a home point with Aston Villa, but followed that up with two misses before the month was out.

Surprisingly, City's fortunes actually worsened in 1952–53. It took a 5–0 home win over Blackpool in the season's penultimate game to ensure City finished one place above relegated Derby and Stoke.

'It was lucky for us that Blackpool had the Cup Final a week later; they didn't look that bothered,' says Paul. 'In the end, it was only our home form that kept us up that year. It was one of those situations where you have a big crowd behind you which helps get your stamina up and helps you play better football.

'It was a funny position for a club like Manchester City to be in. They are a top club; there's none bigger today and there wasn't in my day. People didn't expect us to be down there and with the players we had, I was always confident we could get out of trouble.'

There were some low points on the way. Only 13,562 saw a home win against Stoke; City lost 6–0 to a Cardiff side which had not scored in the previous ten weeks; and in November, Paul was at the heart of a City defence that conceded 12 goals in two games.

He recalls: 'We lost 5–2 at home to Sunderland and I was playing centre-half against Trevor Ford who got four. Then we went to Wolves and lost 7–3. I was marking Roy Swinbourne who got a hat-trick.

'So I had a couple of good games! I didn't get the runaround that often, but those games – especially Sunderland – were embarrassing. After that match, the manager went mad at me and blamed me for the players not being in top condition.

'I shouted back: "That's up to the trainer. I carry the ball out and toss a coin, that's all." The captain did have more responsibilities in my day, but I couldn't be held responsible for everything.'

Ford was just one player with whom Paul enjoyed great confrontations in the 1950s. Another was his Sunderland team-mate Raich Carter. 'A nuisance, a tough player and a great one,' says Roy. 'He used to take the mickey out of me and I'd threaten him: "Do that again and you'll be a spectator!"'

'Wilf Mannion at Middlesbrough was another like that. He wasn't very big, but he had plenty of heart. Hit him and he'd still come back for more.

'As I said, Finney was my most difficult opponent. He could use either foot, go inside or outside and beat you. Matthews would always go outside and keep to the touchline. Not Tom.'

Injuries the following season forced McDowall to make 39 team changes in one eight-week period and a dramatic loss in form saw City again facing a relegation battle in April 1954.

It took a 5–2 home win over Middlesbrough five games from the end of the season for City to ensure their first division safety. For Paul, it was an all too familiar story.

'We got off to a flying start against 'Boro, two goals in as many minutes,' he says. 'When you are in the position we were, players are afraid to make mistakes, but that sort of start settles you down.'

The season also included a bizarre F.A. Cup defeat at home to

Spurs as City players watched and allowed Tottenham's Bennett to tap the ball into their goal, believing him offside! 'Fair dos, though, Spurs played well that day and deserved to win,' says Roy philosophically.

October brought a new experience for Paul and Maine Road – the first game under floodlights. Hearts were the visitors for a friendly match which City won 6–3.

'They were a new venture but I didn't like them,' says Paul. 'In fact, I still don't. In those days they were about as powerful as matchsticks and took some getting used to. And I was a collier!'

The season ended with City fans in uproar against the club's board. Years of profit had not been channelled into improving the side, and the fans had had enough. 'I agreed with the fans,' says Roy. 'The club earned good money through the gates and should have spent it.'

Finally, the board agreed, announcing there was £60,000 for McDowall to spend. A new air of optimism replaced the old lethargy around Maine Road.

By mid-September, a 3–2 win at Arsenal took City to the top of the League. 'What a great feeling that was,' says Roy. 'A young Irish lad Billy McAdams got knocked out but came back to score a great goal that set us on our way.'

City had beaten Arsenal 2–1 at Maine Road earlier in the month. But the Arsenal clashes were costly for Paul.

'Tommy Lawton was playing for them and getting a bit of stick from the crowd, he was coming to the end of his career and wasn't the player he had been,' says Paul.

'A loose ball came over and I said to Dave Ewing, our centre-half: "I'll get this." But Lawton brought his elbow back and knocked four of my teeth out!

'I just couldn't stop the bleeding, though I made it back for the second half. I was trying to get him back but he wasn't falling for it. Eventually, he had to start playing because Arsenal were a goal down.

'The ball came to him and I went right over the top and left six studs in his ankle. You could probably have heard him yelp back in Manchester!

'I'd still have my teeth today if it hadn't been for him. He wasn't

Captain fantastic . . . Paul is chaired by Don Revie as City begin to celebrate their '56 triumph. Note Bert Trautmann, in agony, on the far right.

a particularly dirty player, he was just trying to be a bit clever. Anyway, after the game, I went to see how he was and he called me a dirty beggar. I said: "You're the dirty beggar, look at this," and showed him my mouth.'

City would eventually finish seventh – their best League finish since 1937 – only two points behind runners-up Wolves. They also averaged a higher home attendance than neighbours United for the first time since the war. And there was the huge bonus of a Wembley trip, following a semi-final win over Sunderland.

'I thought the semi should have been cancelled. It was pouring down,' says Roy. 'I was marking Len Shackleton and managed to keep him quiet. At one stage he said to me: "Why don't you get lost and give me a chance."

'Roy Clarke got the only goal, but with a few minutes left he went down with an injured knee. I thought he was acting the goat and picked him up and carried him off the field.

'After the game I told him he had just come off early to get the cheers, but it was a relief when the final whistle went.'

Injury to right-back Jimmy Meadows made sure ten-man City were never in with a real chance at Wembley. Newcastle made a flying start when the great Jackie Milburn headed home from a corner with the game 50 seconds old.

'They had a big centre-forward called Vic Keeble, so I told Dave Ewing to come over and mark him with me. We left Jackie on his own and he got the goal.

'Mind you, it was a terrible corner, straight across goal a couple of yards off the ground. I told Jackie: "You lucky beggar, you never scored. The ball hit you!"

'The papers had a go at me for my tactics after we lost Meadows. They said I should have gone to full-back myself instead of Billy Spurdle, and put Billy at left-half, because he could play anywhere.

'We got murdered down that right-wing, we all had so much running to do. But I was captain and it was my decision. Anyway, if the manager hadn't agreed, he could have done something.

'It was a tremendous disappointment, and at my age I thought my chance of a winner's medal had gone.'

Paul would be back, however, to put that disappointment right after an excellent season in which City took full advantage of the 'Revie Plan'.

With Revie in dispute with McDowall and out of favour for most of the season, his deep-lying centre-forward role went to Johnstone. But, with the Birmingham Final on the horizon, Paul made a case for his team-mate's recall.

'Don hardly played all season, then we went to Eastbourne for a couple of weeks before Wembley, and he was suddenly in the party.

'On the Friday night, Les told me he was thinking of playing him and asked me what I thought. I said: "He's fit and keen, that's half the battle." I agreed he should play.

'All the lads expected Johnny Hart to play, but I knew otherwise. And to be honest, Don had a fair game for us against Birmingham.'

Paul's relationship with McDowall had not always been so harmonious. The pair clashed on a number of occasions.

Explains Roy: 'Les was a very quiet and modest man but I

That Wembley feeling . . . A proud Roy Paul leads City out for the '55 Cup Final, alongside Newcastle's Jimmy Scoular. City became the first team to ever wear tracksuits at a Wembley final!

didn't have the best relationship with him. I liked a drink and that didn't go down well. A number of times, the chairman Bob Smith had to come to my assistance.

'Eventually, I said to Les: "Judge me by what I do on a Saturday, not whether or not I have a drink during the week." He couldn't argue with that and he never mentioned it again.'

Paul was part of a City side that played as hard off the field as it did on it; as fellow Welsh international and roommate Roy Clarke discovered more than once.

'Roy was tea-total but we dragged him out for a drink once,' says Paul. 'He was on shandies but when it came to his round, we all hit the double whiskies. He never drank with us again after that!'

By the time of that '56 triumph, Paul's international career had reached its conclusion. His 33 caps included a single goal in a 5–1 win over Belgium – 'A blind man could have scored it,' says Roy. 'The keeper saved Roy Clarke's shot and I was on the line.'

The highlight had come in his final season of international football. His eighth and last meeting with England brought a 2–1 win at Cardiff, his only victory against the old enemy.

'I will always remember our second goal. I beat Nat Lofthouse in the air, and instead of going to the right, I went straight up the middle, and crossed to the far post where Cliff Jones headed the winner.

'I got carried off the field that day, a great memory. But Wales had a pretty poor side in my day. We had some good players, but some average ones as well.'

Paul's City career did not finish on such a high note. The season after the Wembley victory brought a familiar flirtation with relegation. Only a successful run in late March ensured City would finish as high as 18th.

By the summer of '57, the 37-year-old Paul decided to retire.

'City offered me another contract, but I was starting to get caught on the field,' he says. 'I used to be able to get away from most players. When I couldn't anymore, I decided it was time to quit.'

Paul's football career wound down with two seasons as player-manager at non-league Worcester City. In spite of successes such as guiding them to an F.A. Cup fourth round tie with Sheffield United, he eventually found the strain of commuting from South Wales too great.

He returned to his beloved Valleys to work as a lorry driver though, predictably, Paul had the last laugh over football.

'Worcester had bought me a car for all the travelling and asked for it back when I quit,' he explains. 'But I knew I was going to be leaving and had already sold it. I got £500 for it!'

Paul is still far from forgotten at Maine Road, although he is only an occasional visitor to his old club. Team-mate Ken Barnes is a regular caller and travelled to the Rhondda Valley in 1990 when Paul received an award for services to Welsh sport.

'Ken keeps inviting me back, saying they would love to see me at City,' says Roy. 'One day I'll make it, but I don't know. I have to admit, I just don't like football nowadays.'

Roy Paul
FULL INTERNATIONAL CAPS—33
(9 with Swansea, 24 with Manchester City – 1 goal)

(Wales score given first)
1948: Scotland (Cardiff) 1–3, England (Villa Park) 0–1.
1949: Northern Ireland (Belfast) 2–0, Portugal (Lisbon) 2–3, Switzerland (Berne) 0–4, England (Cardiff) 1–4, Scotland (Hampden) 0–2, Belgium (Cardiff) 5–1 GOAL.
1950: Northern Ireland (Wrexham) 0–0, Scotland (Cardiff) 1–3, England (Sunderland) 2–4.
1951: Northern Ireland (Cardiff) 2–1, Portugal (Cardiff) 2–1, Switzerland (Wrexham) 3–2, England (Cardiff) 1–1, Scotland (Hampden) 1–0, Rest of UK (Cardiff) 3–2.
1952: Northern Ireland (Swansea) 3–0, Scotland (Cardiff) 1–2, England (Wembley) 2–5.
1953: Northern Ireland (Belfast) 3–2, France (Paris) 1–6, Yugoslavia (Belgrade) 2–5, England (Cardiff) 1–4, Scotland (Hampden) 3–3.
1954: Northern Ireland (Wrexham) 1–2, Yugoslavia (Cardiff) 1–3, Scotland (Cardiff) 0–1, England (Wembley) 2–3.
1955: England (Cardiff) 2–1, Scotland (Hampden) 0–2, Austria (Wrexham) 1–2, Northern Ireland (Cardiff) 1–1.

MANCHESTER CITY APPEARANCES

League: 270, 9 goals. F.A. Cup: 23, 0 goals. TOTAL: 293, 9 goals.

CHAPTER FOUR

Bobby Johnstone

'It was a simple goal really,' says Bobby Johnstone recollecting the strike that took him into the F.A. Cup history books. 'Bert Trautmann kicked the ball out, Jack Dyson helped it on, I ran onto it and stuck it away. Pretty simple.'

Johnstone's flash of characteristically effective finishing came midway through the second half of the 1956 Final and cemented City's 3–1 win over Birmingham.

Roy Paul, the captain who had promised City fans they would return to Wembley in the wake of the disappointing Final loss to Newcastle 12 months earlier, strode up to collect the trophy.

Trautmann, the brilliant German goalkeeper nursed a painful injury, unaware that he had in fact broken his neck and would be out of football for seven months.

And Johnstone, an inside forward of dazzling skill, had become a part of Wembley folklore – the first player to score in consecutive Wembley Finals.

It was a fairytale finale for a fairytale side, never far away from controversy and blessed with some of the finest footballers of the day.

That May afternoon in '56 had seen City make a dream start with Joe Hayes scoring after three minutes. Birmingham's Noel Kinsey equalised 11 minutes later, setting the scene for Johnstone to spark City into life in the second period.

'I had a hand in the second goal, slipping it through for Jack Dyson who turned and whacked it in,' says Bobby. 'Then, a couple of minutes later, I got the third and it was pretty comfortable after that.

'It was certainly an advantage for us, going back to Wembley after losing there the previous year, and I think that was the best we played all season – certainly in the cup games.

Wembley bound . . . Johnstone turns in delight after hitting the winner in the F.A. Cup sixth round against Everton in 1956.

'But the thing everyone remembers the game for was Bert's injury. Of course, no-one had the faintest idea he was that badly hurt. Not even when we had the banquet that night at the Cafe Royal.

'It was a great feeling to have that winner's medal – especially after the disappointment the year before – and to score in successive finals made it even more special.'

City's cup winning story revolved around injuries – and not only Trautmann's. Johnstone recalls that City were almost denied his own match-winning exploits.

'I was struggling with a knee injury right up until the Friday,' he explains. 'In fact I wouldn't have played if Billy Spurdle had been fit. But Billy had boils under his arm, they spread and he could hardly move.

'Don Revie had not played much all year because he had fallen out with the management earlier in the season; he came in at centre-forward and I took Billy's place at outside-right.

'It was the first time I'd ever played there and I was still feeling my injury – I wore a bandage in the first half.'

In addition, right-back Bill Leivers played with a suspect ankle, sprained two weeks earlier. It was hardly ideal preparation for a City team that had been far from convincing on the run to Wembley.

The seeds of the Cup Final triumph, recalls Johnstone, had been planted immediately after City's defeat at the hands of a talented Newcastle side in the 1955 Final.

'We came home to Manchester after that and were invited to the Lord Mayor's place for a reception,' he remembers. 'Roy Paul stepped up to the microphone and causally announced that we would go back and win it next year!

'My attitude was that lightning wouldn't strike twice. And, sure enough, our cup form the following season was very poor – we hardly won a game on merit in '55–56.'

The road to Wembley started at home to Blackpool, a game locked at 1–1 until it was abandoned through fog – 'I'm sure Blackpool would have won that first game if it had gone the full 90 minutes, they scored after ten seconds!' says Bobby.

'We won the re-arranged game 2–1, I scored one of them, and won 1–0 at Southend in the next round. That game should never have been played. The pitch was like a beach, and we scraped a 1–0 win through Johnny Hart. Mind you, it took him about six kicks to get the ball over the line as it stuck in the mud.'

Liverpool visited Maine Road in the fifth round, a 0–0 draw that City could again count themselves fortunate not to lose. The Anfield replay surely looked to be the point at which City's dreams would end.

'We went 1–0 down, but Dyson equalised and, very late in the game, Joe Hayes gave us the lead,' says Johnstone. 'Then with the last kick of the game Billy Liddle scored what looked like Liverpool's equaliser.

'But the referee had already blown for full time and it was disallowed. That was the sort of cup luck we had all that season!'

Liverpool's neighbours Everton deserved to exact revenge for Merseyside in the quarter-finals at Maine Road. But in spite of their total dominance, the visitors only led 1–0 at the interval.

'They absolutely tanned us, it should have been 4–0,' says Johnstone. 'Then we scored twice in the second half – I headed the winner from Roy Clarke's left-wing cross. It was one of

Johnstone (front row fourth from left) with the Great Britain team to face the Rest of Europe in 1955. City team mate Don Revie is fourth from left on the back row.

my most memorable goals, in front of over 76,000!'

As had been the case 12 months earlier, the semi-final took City to Villa Park. This time Spurs provided the opposition and – hardly surprising – Johnstone considered his side lucky to get through. That they did was thanks to Johnstone himself.

'We won 1–0 and I scored the goal – an exact copy of the Everton goal. Clarkey crossed and I dived in at the far post. But we were fortunate again, they had a strong penalty appeal turned down in the last minute.'

Johnstone was a key figure in City's consecutive Wembley appearances in 1955 and '56, signing from Scottish club Hibernian shortly before the 1955 semi-final with Sunderland.

'It was a hard decision to come to Manchester after spending most of my life in Scotland, but I soon realised it was the right one,' says Bobby, who was 25 when City manager Les McDowall paid Hibs £22,000.

'City had a lot of good players at the time – Paul, Clarke, Revie, Trautmann. It looked a good side on paper and a good challenge for me. And I was impressed with the set-up, a nice ground to play on, and a good spirit around the club.

'These were the days of the maximum wage and I signed for the princely sum of £20 a week. There was £4 a win, £2 a draw and something like £15 for internationals, though I could never understand why we were paid for an honour like that.'

54

Johnstone, raised in Selkirk, signed for Hibs after shining in a five-a-side tournament at the age of 17. He represented the Army during National Service days in the late 1940s and, after being stationed at Edinburgh Castle, was given the opportunity to make his Hibs debut in a League Cup tie with Partick Thistle at the age of 19.

He quickly became part of the most successful side in Hibs history, and a key member of the most feared forward line Scottish football has ever known – the 'Famous Five'.

Says Johnstone: 'That was the best forward line I ever played in. Five Scotland internationals – myself, Gordon Smith, Lawrie Reilly, Eddie Turnbull and Willie Ormond.

'We won three titles in five years and had some incredible matches. Rangers were our big rivals; I remember playing them in the last game of 1953 in front of over 100,000 at Ibrox.

'It ended 0–0, although Willie hit the post in the last few minutes, and we lost the title on goal average. I had nine good seasons at Hibs but by 1955 they were short of money, and out of the Scottish Cup, when City came in.'

City swooped to sign Johnstone – a Scotland regular by this stage – although the move did not go down well with one of McDowall's close rivals.

'I know Matt Busby wasn't very pleased when I moved to City,' says Bobby. 'He had played for Hibs in war-time football and the club promised him first refusal if any of the forward line were for sale.

'I don't know if it was coincidence, but Hibs used to play Manchester United regularly in friendlies. When I went to City, they stopped!'

A Hayes hat-trick ensured Johnstone's City career got off to a winning start in a 4–2 victory over Bolton. Tragedy struck in the following game – a goalless draw at Huddersfield – when Johnny Hart suffered a badly broken leg, an injury that effectively ended his career, and guaranteed Johnstone a place in the line-up for the Villa Park semi with Sunderland.

'That match should never have been played, the pitch was under water,' says Bobby. 'We stayed overnight in Birmingham and it poured down all the time we were there.

The all-rounder . . . Johnstone indulging in his other sporting love, cricket. City team mate Jack Dyson, a professional cricketer with Lancashire, gives him some tips.

'The game only went ahead because all the Sunderland supporters had come down from the North-east. They were a good side, with players like Len Shackleton, but the conditions didn't suit good football.

'It must have been one of the poorest semis in history. Roy Clarke scored the only goal early in the second half then went off with a cartilage injury.

'Poor Clarkey couldn't play in the Final, but for me it was a great feeling to get to a Cup Final. I had lost to Motherwell in a League Cup Final, but for all our success, we never got to a Scottish F.A. Cup Final at Hibs.'

With Clarke and Hart out of the meeting with Newcastle, City faced an uphill struggle. It became almost insurmountable by the 20th minute when the Blues, already a goal down, lost full-back Jimmy Meadows with a knee injury.

'Jackie Milburn gave them the lead inside a minute and we were unfortunate to lose Jimmy,' says Johnstone. 'People had talked about introducing substitutes into football for years but had never got around to doing it.

'So we were down to ten men which was also unfortunate from a spectators' point of view; it was less of a game with ten men against 11.'

Nevertheless, Johnstone made sure Newcastle had to battle to win the trophy, beating United keeper Ronnie Simpson – a former National Service pal – just before halftime.

'It was one of the best goals I ever scored,' he says. 'I knocked it out to Joe Hayes who crossed it fairly low, I dived and headed it from about 12 yards. As soon as I hit it I knew Ronnie was going to be picking that one out!

'Just after that, I made myself a chance, dribbling through. Ronnie came rushing out and I hit it against his legs. I should have made it 2–2 and made a game of it. As it was, we had no right-back in the second half and Bobby Mitchell had an easy afternoon down that wing for Newcastle.'

City's 3–1 defeat was hard for most of Johnstone's team-mates to stomach. For Johnstone and wing-half Ken Barnes, it was the long faces at the City function that evening that were too much to stomach.

'We ended up going to Newcastle's celebration,' admits Bobby. 'My attitude was once the final whistle went, the game was over. Ken and I sat with Jimmy Scoular, the Newcastle captain, and had a great night.'

Under McDowall's guidance, City would be back to win the trophy 12 months later and, in spite of the disappointment of Wembley defeat, Johnstone felt very optimistic about the future as he spent the summer of 1955 engaged in playing his great love – cricket.

'The manager's job was completely different then to what it is today,' says Johnstone. 'Les was very unorthodox and had some very funny ideas.

Signing on . . . Johnstone arriving at Manchester station to sign for City from Hibernian in March 1955.

'He introduced deep-lying centre-forwards and spoke to me about doing things like having a front-line made up entirely of inside-forwards. I don't think that particular tactic would have worked but I welcomed talking to him. Les enjoyed the game and put everything into it, he was a good man to work for.'

McDowall's most famous innovation was the so-called Revie Plan. Though by no means original, it still proved highly efficient when it was introduced in the season Johnstone arrived at Maine Road.

Explains Bobby: 'The Hungarians had first used it, and murdered England at Wembley playing that way. It basically involved the centre-forward – Revie – playing deep and combining with the wing-halves.

'They had tried it in the reserves before I came and persevered with it. As long as you had someone who could play a bit at

Bobby and team mate Joe Hayes indulging in some unusual pre-Wembley training in 1956.

centre-forward, you had a chance of getting away with it.

'The ball was struck for other players to run onto and the idea was to have four attackers, instead of three, to try and catch the centre-half out. Most clubs found it difficult to play against because they weren't sure what was going on.

'When Don fell out with the club the following season, I played the deep-lying centre-forward position and found it easy. I seemed to see a lot more of the ball and be more involved, which suited me.'

Some of McDowall's innovations were nowhere near as successful. In 1957–58, he introduced the 'dual centre-half' plan.

Although most teams would play with two centre-halves in a back four by the 1960s, this particular scheme – involving Dave Ewing and Keith Marsden – was too far ahead of its time.

'It was a silly plan and Les was going to use it against Preston who had some great players like Tom Finney and Tommy Docherty. I'm glad to say I didn't play because we lost 6–1.

'I was left out for the next game as well. We continued with two centre-halves at West Brom . . . and lost 9–2! Two games and 15 goals against.'

Surprisingly, City finished fifth that season as they became the first club to score and concede 100 goals in the same season. But F.A. Cup heroics aside, City's League form was disappointingly inconsistent during Johnstone's five years at Maine Road.

'The season we won the cup, we finished fourth but, although we were always thereabouts, we let it slip after winning the semi-final, which often happens.

'I don't think we had a good squad at the time and although we were quite confident the following season, we didn't realise how much we were going to miss Bert, who was recovering from his broken neck.

'We finished 18th and Bert's absence was the main reason. Clubs had also sussed out the Revie Plan, but Bert missed the first half of the season and his replacements – George Thompson and John Savage – weren't really up to it.

'Bert had been the dominant man for so long that the defence found it difficult when someone else came in. It was a bit depressing.'

One extraordinary match in that 1956–57 season seemed to sum up City's Jekyll and Hyde character. Leading Newcastle 3–0 at half-time of an F.A. Cup third round replay, City somehow snatched defeat from the jaws of victory, going out 5–4 in extra-time!

'It was one of the greatest games I ever played in but was typical of what we were like at that time,' says Johnstone. 'I headed our second and, at half-time, I remember fans talking about how much it was going to cost them to get to Millwall in the next round.

'But it was probably the worst game I ever saw Bert have – not

Bobby (front left) at Bert Trautmann's testimonial dinner in April 1964. A fresh-faced and pipe-smoking Denis Law is at the rear on the far left.

that it was all his fault. If Billy McAdams had taken every chance that came his way in the first half, he would have re-written the record books. He should have had six!

'They got back to 3–3, then we took the lead again in extra-time when I got another header. Roy Little gave the ball away for Len White to make it 4–4 then Len got the winner with a couple of minutes left.

'Even then, we could have made it 5–5 but Jack Dyson hit the post with the last kick of the game when it would have been easier to score. There were 47,000 there that day – for a Wednesday afternoon game – and they certainly got their money's worth.'

For Johnstone, '56–57 brought him his third and last City

hat-trick in a crucial 4–1 win at Cardiff in March. He had netted another that term, in a typically high-scoring 5–4 win over Chelsea. His first had come against Portsmouth in the previous season.

Johnstone's close pal Ken Barnes remembers that New Year's Day performance against Pompey particularly well.

'Bob had been enjoying himself the night before and came in stinking of booze,' recalls Ken. 'He asked me to keep the trainer away from him and I gave him a right roasting.

'Then he went out and scored a hat-trick – all with his head. I said afterwards: "You should get drunk before every game if that's what you do!" '

With Trautmann gradually playing his way back to form in '56–57, that Johnstone-inspired win at Cardiff helped ensure City held onto their First Division status in readiness for the extraordinary goal-packed season that was to follow.

As well as the gaudy scorelines from Preston and West Brom, Johnstone scored twice in an 8–4 defeat at Leicester and played his part in a 6–2 win against Everton. City either scored or conceded four goals in 20 of their 43 League and Cup games that season!

One such match – a 5–2 home win against Chelsea – is remembered by Johnstone for another reason. It produced the only sending-off of his career.

'It was such a ridiculous decision, McDowall thought I had come off to change my boots,' laughs Bobby. 'Their inside-forward was backing into Ken Barnes from kick-outs, so I told Ken to stand a bit away from him, then run in and hit him!

'The ref heard this and sent me off for inciting a teammate! I was in the bath when McDowall came in and told me he thought I had just come off to change boots.

'I told him the ref would send one of their players off to even things up and the next thing we heard was the sound of a player's boots running into their dressing room. Sure enough, he had sent Ian MacFarlane off for the first foul he committed.

'That was a crazy season all round. But with Bert back to his best, we could have been knocking on the door if we hadn't experimented with so many crazy plans early on. Les had too many plans in his head sometimes, he used to get players mixed up! I think if we had left the Revie Plan alone it would have worked out.'

Sadly, things would only get worse for Johnstone in the 12 remaining months of his City career. The 1958–59 season saw the Scotsman battling against knee injuries, a legacy of the F.A. Cup winning season, and the club's form reflected Johnstone's own.

'We started the season well, I scored a couple in a 4–3 win against Burnley,' he recalls. 'But it was hard to get a regular pattern going. There was my injury; and the forward line was breaking up a bit.'

Fortunately for City, Johnstone was fit for the final six games of the season, including a crucial clash with Leicester on the final day. After seven defeats and two draws in their previous nine games, City entertained Leicester aiming to avoid joining Portsmouth in relegation to division two.

As fate would have it, Aston Villa – led by a promising young manager called Joe Mercer – were level on points with City and had to visit West Brom on that tense April evening.

'I've played in cup finals, internationals and other very important games, but this is the one that stands out for me,' says Johnstone.

'There were 47,000 there for a night game and, although the outcome meant it was a fabulous match to play in, it was one of the worst I've ever known for nerves.

'They scored early on and things weren't helped by the fact that Villa had kicked off a quarter of an hour before us and their score was put up every 15 minutes.

'Luckily, in spite of our position, we could still count on some good players and we came back to win 3–1. It was just as well because Villa were winning 1–0 for most of the game. That would have put us down, but West Brom got a late equaliser to make us safe in any case.'

Three games and one goal into 1959–60, Johnstone left Maine Road, returning to Hibs in a £7,000 deal. For a City career that had started in such glorious fashion, it was a downbeat conclusion.

'To be honest, we had used so many plans under Les that the

players were getting fed up,' he confesses. 'I thought if someone came in for me, I'd go. I'd had enough of all the chopping and changing.'

Considering the talent – including Johnstone – around Maine Road in the late 1950s, the lack of success is hard to fathom.

'We had a good mixture,' he confirms. 'Bert was the best goal-keeper I've ever seen in my life, Ken Barnes a cultured footballer at right-half, Roy Paul a good footballer and hard with it, Dave Ewing a strong centre-half. You can go right through the team.'

Johnstone's admiration for his captain, Paul, is understand-able. It did not, however, extend to the international arena, as Paul discovered in a Scotland-Wales meeting in 1955.

'He was left-half, I was at inside-right and we won 2–0 at Hampden. I scored both goals and when I went back to Maine Road the next day I hung some carrots on Roy's peg.

'His favourite insult for an opponent was to call him a "don-key" so I put these carrots there with a note saying" To be eaten on Blackpool beach!"

'You could have some fun with Roy, he was a great character and probably the best player I played with at City. He was worth that title for his captaincy alone. And I only saw him in his thirties – goodness knows what he was like as a young man.'

Johnstone's international career was highly successful. Ten goals in 17 appearances from the time he scored on his debut in a 3–2 win over England in 1951.

'That was a funny game, I could have had a hat-trick in the first 20 minutes,' says Bobby. 'But Willie Waddell, the Rangers player, just told me to carry on and forget about the misses.

'I thumped one in from 15 yards to make it 1–1, but England were unlucky to lose Wilf Mannion with a broken jaw. Mind you, they got their own back, I was in the side that lost 7–2 to them at Wembley in '55.

'Even that wasn't the best team I played against. The Hungarians came to Hampden a year after they had destroyed England at Wembley. They were the best side I ever saw and we did well only to lose 4–2. I had the consolation of scoring one of our goals – a header – and got a set of golf clubs for being Scotland's man of the match.'

International duty . . . The Scottish forward line to take on England in 1956.
Graham Leggat (Aberdeen), Johnstone, Laurie Reilly (Hibs), Ian McMillan
(Airdrie), Gordon Smith (Hibs).

His Maine Road career over, Johnstone only spent a year with
Hibs before returning to Lancashire and fourth division Oldham.

Says Johnstone: 'It was smashing there, a homely little club
with a few ex-City players.

'They were averaging about 4,000 crowds, but they got 17,000
for my first game so it was nice to bring people back through the
turnstiles. More importantly, we got promotion to the third so I
think the manager Jack Rowley considered the £5,000 he paid for
me a good investment.'

After five years at Oldham, Johnstone retired in 1965, aged 36.
He still lives in Hollinwood between Oldham and Manchester,
and played cricket for the town team until his 50th birthday. After
football, the Scotsman worked for an engineering firm for 15
years and nowadays is content with work on Manchester's
Smithfield Market.

A regular visitor with his old pal Ken Barnes to Maine Road, together they helped launch a former players' association in early 1991.

The accent may still be unmistakably Scottish, but it is easy to detect where Johnstone's heart lies.

'I was quite sad to leave City, I had made so many friends at the club and in Manchester,' he confesses. The fondness is mutual.

In spite of only making 124 League appearances for the Blues, there cannot be many dissenting voices when his name is put forward as one of City's post-war greats.

Johnstone himself modestly sums up his abilities: 'I had reasonable skill and was fairly fast over a dozen yards, but was more a goal provider than a goal getter.

'My philosophy was that football was meant to be entertainment and, although I could still take chances, my main aim was making goals.

'The pleasing thing is that wherever I played, the centre-forwards I played with broke club records. There was Reilly in my first spell with Hibs, Joe Hayes at City, Joe Baker in my second spell at Hibs, and Bert Lister at Oldham. It happened four times, so I can't have done that badly . . .'

Bobby Johnstone
FULL INTERNATIONAL CAPS – 17
(13 with Hibernian, 4 with Manchester City – 10 goals)

(Scotland score given first)
1951: England (Wembley) 3–2 GOAL, Denmark (Glasgow) 3–1, France (Glasgow) 1–0, Northern Ireland (Glasgow) 3–0 TWO GOALS.
1952: England (Glasgow) 1–2.
1953: England (Wembley) 2–2, Sweden (Glasgow) 1–2 GOAL, Wales (Glasgow) 3–3 GOAL.
1954: England (Glasgow) 2–4, Norway (Glasgow) 1–0, Finland (Helsinki) 2–1 GOAL, Northern Ireland (Glasgow) 2–2 GOAL, Hungary (Glasgow) 2–4 GOAL.

1955:   England (Wembley) 2–7, Northern Ireland (Belfast) 1–2,
Wales (Glasgow) 1–1.

MANCHESTER CITY APPEARANCES

League: 124, 42 goals. F.A. Cup: 14, 9 goals. TOTAL: 138, 51 goals.

CHAPTER FIVE

Mike Summerbee

Days before the start of the 1965–66 season, Manchester City's new manager Joe Mercer made his first signing for the club, handing over £35,000 to Swindon Town for a fresh-faced forward called Mike Summerbee.

The City manager knew Summerbee well. Mercer had played alongside his father, George, in war-time football with Aldershot and had followed the youngster's career since he was 15.

Summerbee, 22-years-old, was spending the summer of '65 in Torquay, working on deck chairs, scraping a few bob together and passing time with Torquay footballers John Bond and John Benson, two names that would feature prominently at Maine Road in years to come as managers of the club.

It was from Benson's back garden that Summerbee made the most important step of his footballing life by accepting Mercer's invitation to join him in the North-west.

It was an invitation, Summerbee soon realised, that was heaven sent.

'As soon as I drove into Manchester, I could sense something about the place,' recalls Summerbee.

'Even though City were in the second division, they were a huge club. The ground is an awe-inspiring place; it reeks of tradition and great players.

'Although I could not compare City to anything I had known before, I soon realised what a privilege and pleasure it is to be able to play for a club like that.'

In short, the extrovert and hugely gifted Summerbee and Manchester City were made for each other. The only piece remaining in the equation required Summerbee to win over the City supporters. There, Summerbee already had a head start.

He explains: 'I had played at Maine Road with Swindon the

season before and we had really ripped City to pieces. I scored as
well, so the fans remembered me.

'I think northern supporters generally have a very good judg-
ment of the game. They certainly know "kidders" when they see
them. If you have just a moderate amount of ability and are
prepared to work hard, you have a great opportunity.'

Summerbee succeeded on both counts, quickly playing his way
into City folklore. Even in a day when talented players and
'characters' seemed to abound, the exhilarating performances
and antics of the man made him stand out.

In one sense, he was a victim of his time, performing in an age
when wingers were a dirty word in international football. The
eight caps he won were scant reward in comparison to a plethora
of contemporaries who made many more England appearances
on a fraction of the ability.

But in another sense, Summerbee could not have timed his
emergence in English football better. Alongside Colin Bell, Francis Lee and the other members of the Joe Mercer-Malcolm
Allison dynasty, Summerbee mesmerized supporters and defenders alike.

In yet another sense, he was ahead of his time. In an age when
wingers were almost morally obliged to spend their time on the
receiving end of the near-homicidal attention of opposing fullbacks, Summerbee broke the mould. He preferred to strike early.
Retaliation is more effective if you get it in first!

'People always called me a dirty player, but I was simply trying
to survive,' he says. 'As a forward I used to take a lot of stick, so
I dished it out as well.

'It was alright to be a defender and be hard, but forwards
weren't supposed to be. In any case, it was all good humoured.

'I would tread on a defender's toes or something like that, and
the game would always end with a shake of the hand and a pint
afterwards. That was what it was like playing in my day.

'And I never broke anyone's leg – I just broke my own a couple
of times!'

Summerbee had not always been so competent in the selfpro-
tection department. Indeed, he can trace an instant change in his
style to a game in his Swindon days.

Kings of Europe . . . Summerbee (front row far right) pictured with the City side the day before the Cup Winners' Cup date with Gornik Zabrze. The line-up (back row left to right) Allison, Booth, Doyle, Pardoe, Corrigan, Dowd, Oakes, Donachie, Ewing. (front row) Towers, Carradous, Bowyer, Bell, Book, Lee, Young, Summerbee. Sadly, Mike would miss the Final through injury.

'I remember it clearly. We were playing Notts County and I was only about 19,' he says.

'I had pulled out of three or four tackles and at half-time the manager, Bert Head, pointed to me in front of a dressing room full of these hardened pros and said: "If you do that one more time, you'll never play for me again."

'He told me to close my eyes, get stuck in and I wouldn't get hurt. It's down to him I am the way I am!'

That attitude would serve City well in countless difficult situations in the coming years, not least of all when Mercer's fledgling side were trying to find their feet in the brutal world of the first division. One anecdote sums up Summerbee's value to the Blues.

'It was our first season in the first and we were really up against it at Chelsea one day,' says Summerbee.

'We weren't the most attractive side at the time, there was a small crowd and the game was rubbish. All the Chelsea hard men were playing – Harris, Boyle, Osgood, Hinton, McCreadie – and I gave the keeper Peter Bonetti "one".

'Within seconds, they were all around me, shoving and pushing.

I said, "Look, you've got 60 minutes left to do me, but if I go, I'm taking two of you with me!"

'They went crazy and spent the rest of the game rushing around chasing me. They forgot all about the football and we got away with a 0–0 draw!'

Summerbee had been born with a fine football pedigree. His father had been a member of Preston's great pre-War team and Mike was born in the Lancashire town in December 1942, moving to Cheltenham at the age of six when George became manager of the local non-league side.

A trial with Bristol City came to nothing because of Summerbee's homesickness, and the youngster settled down to life as an office boy in an aircraft factory until he caught the eye of Swindon Town's chief scout Cecil Green, who would later become the club's chairman.

At the age of 16, Summerbee made his debut in the third division, becoming a regular in the first Swindon side ever to win promotion, in 1963. The Wiltshire club only remained in the second division for two seasons before suffering relegation and Summerbee, 22 yet with 300 games already behind him, was attracting attention.

'Spurs bid £12,000 for me which was turned down; Leicester were also interested and Joe actually tried to sign me when he was manager at Aston Villa,' says Summerbee.

'Eventually, Swindon agreed to sell me and, even though I was no stranger to the second division, I was a bit overawed playing for a great club like City and with such great players.'

It didn't take the precocious forward long to settle down. On his debut at Middlesbrough, Summerbee's cross set up Jimmy Murray for City's goal in a 1–1 draw.

City lost just five times all season on the way to the 1965–66 second division championship, with Summerbee an ever-present on the right-wing.

The first division, however, was to prove a slightly harder proposition – for a time at least.

'We murdered the second division with the side Malcolm and Joe were building, but we didn't make an immediate impact on the first,' says Mike.

'We signed Colin Bell just before promotion, and Tony Book came in the close season, but for a while we were trying to feel our way. For me, the key to the door, the man who bound the whole thing together was Francis Lee.

'We had match winners throughout the side, but Franny was the renowned goalscorer, the man who – along with Neil Young – could provide the goals to win matches out of nothing.'

Summerbee himself, playing centre-forward, was an integral part of that most exhilarating of forward lines. Gradually, Mercer's side was emerging as true Championship contenders.

'We suddenly woke up that season; the difference was the confidence in our own ability,' he explains. 'City had been trod on for years and everyone was used to United being top dogs.

'Everyone expected us to go straight down after promotion, but here we were fighting our way back. We were a superb team – and I mean a team.

'The club had changed, almost overnight, and that was all down to Malcolm and Joe. I could understand why United players walked ten feet tall when they got off a coach behind Matt Busby. Joe had the same effect on us, a great figurehead loved by everybody.

'Malcolm was a flamboyant and great coach. His obvious mistake was pressing to get into management. If he had stuck to the coaching, he would have been involved with England by now. A brilliant coach.'

The season finale took Mercer, Allison et al to Newcastle for a match they had to win to guarantee the title. The scene was set for this extraordinary City side's the finest hour.

'I remember everything about the whole game,' says Mike. 'Myself, Colin Bell and Peter Blakey the physio travelled up on our own on the train because Colin and I were both nursing injuries.

'We arrived at our usual hotel in Gateshead, had a meal and a few bottles of wine and slinked off to bed about 11. The atmosphere was so relaxed, but I remember waking up about ten the next morning with this roar outside the hotel.

'The road was just choc-a-bloc with City supporters in cars with their hooters going; there must have been 500 outside our hotel.

But the atmosphere was still brilliant, no trace of nerves.

'We were looking forward to it, though we knew Newcastle had a good side and by the time we got to the changing room the tension was growing. The dressing room was full of people, but ten minutes before kick-off, the boss cleared everyone out apart from the players and the backroom staff.

'I think Joe's team talk amounted to "Get out there and sort it out!" '

With those prophetic words ringing in their ears, City got off to a dream start – courtesy of Summerbee.

'It was a lovely day and, while the surface was good on the wings and in the middle, it was bumpy in the goalmouths.

'After about ten minutes, this ball came through from the right. If it had been a flat surface, I would have struggled to score, but as Willie McFaul came out of his goal, the ball bobbled and I was able to flick it over him.'

The Geordies were determined to make City toil for their title. Pop Robson immediately put United level and Neil Young's magnificent volley was cancelled out by a second equaliser by Jackie Sinclair.

'It was 2–2 at half-time and our defence was scared stiff,' says Summerbee. 'We went back into the dressing room and Malcolm tore into them, telling them to tighten up.

'They did brilliantly in the second half and another goal from Neil Young and one from Franny wrapped it up, even though they pulled one back near the end.

'I remember sitting in this lovely hot bath after the game and the first thing I thought about was a bet I had made about four weeks before the end of the season. You could get 20–1 on us to win the League so I'd had a flutter and won £200!

'That was a lot of money then. There I was, sitting back, thinking "Blimey, I've won £200 here!" '

That result and the attendant League title meant far more, of course. For City fans, used to playing second fiddle to the reds from the other side of town, it marked a long-awaited upturn in fortune for the Maine Road club.

Summerbee acknowledges that. 'Personally, I never played football for medals. The most satisfying thing for me was putting Manchester City back on the map.

The boss . . . Summerbee in charge at Stockport in November 1978.

'It didn't particularly matter that it was at United's expense because there was never any animosity between the two sets of players.

'What did matter was that our Championship gave City their credibility back and meant our fans could walk down streets with their heads held up. Looking back, that's what gave me greatest pleasure.'

Summerbee had become a key part of a city resurgent on the football field and off it. As well as dominating the English football scene, Manchester was leading the way in fashion, music and nightlife. And Summerbee and some of his colleagues were very much at the centre of that 'scene'.

'It was an incredible era. United had won the European Cup that season, so you can imagine what Manchester was like,' he says.

'We had a voodoo on United; I think they only beat us once in the League in about seven years and in every derby game there would be near enough 22 internationals on display.

'If people were interested in individuals, there was always Lee, Bell, Summerbee, Law, Best, Charlton; but City's big success was always the team spirit Malcolm created.

'We were hard-drinking and hard-training. We had the fittest side in the League and our confidence and camaraderie stemmed from the way we lived. Malcolm would take us away for weekends and tours to get this team spirit going. I don't think you can have real camaraderie if you go your separate ways after work every day. Sometimes you need to live in each other's pockets.'

One pocket Summerbee often found himself living in belonged to his close friend from across the city, George Best.

'We still have a great friendship that dates back to my early days at City,' says Mike. 'We used to have some great times and, whatever people might say, George is still a great fellow.

'He looked great off the field and playing against Bestie was like nothing on earth. He stood above everyone else. There will never be anyone else like him in my lifetime.

'Manchester was buzzing in those days with the discos and the clubs. Me and Bestie would do a dozen on a Saturday night and still be playing cards at four in the morning. Wonderful!

'But we were so fit, we could get away with it. It was an attitude of mind. As young people, we used to have a good life and if it ever affected our football, well, I wasn't aware of it.'

The honours that came flooding City's way in the coming seasons suggest that was the case. Summerbee does have one confession to make concerning City's surprisingly unconvincing defence of their League title, however.

'Quite simply, we got over-confident,' he admits. 'I was playing centre-forward and thought I was the only man who could play that position.

'I ended up struggling; subconsciously I had lowered my standards. We all thought we were unbeatable and lost that edge.'

Instead, City channelled their proven talent into cup winning performances. First on the honours list was the 1969 F.A. Cup, thanks to a 1–0 victory over relegation-bound Leicester.

'It was an enjoyable day, but it all happened so quickly,' says Mike. 'I don't remember much about it – except we were a bit lucky.

'We should have buried them in the first 20 minutes, but they had a few chances as well. I managed to cross for Neil Young to get another vital goal. But the most memorable part was the homecoming.

'We were anxious, thinking no-one would show up. We caught a train to Wilmslow to take an open-top bus and there were hundreds of people lining the route into town. Fans had even painted their houses blue and white.'

Within 12 months, City were back at Wembley in the Final of the League Cup against West Bromwich Albion. Again, it is an occasion Summerbee remembers for slightly strange reasons.

'On the Wednesday before the game we drew 0–0 in the Cup Winners' Cup against Academica Coimbra in Portugal. It was about 80 degrees, but on the flight back, we were diverted from London to Birmingham because of snow.

'We got a coach back to our Wembley base and I remember stopping on a motorway at 2 a.m. for bacon sandwiches, a couple of days before a cup final!

'We didn't even train before the Final and it was a complete contrast in conditions. Wembley was awful with the snow; and the Horse of the Year show had been held on it shortly before.

'We won 2–1 in extra-time, which I missed because I got a hairline fracture of my leg. The ball stuck in all the mud and Ray Wilson caught me – it was nobody's fault.'

That injury would sadly cost Summerbee another cup winning appearance as City lifted the European Cup Winners' Cup in Vienna in April.

'I played against Sheffield United a few days before the Final and got whacked again which meant me missing the game. It's a good job I did, they didn't miss me.'

Summerbee's ever-present record in the run to the Final earned him a winner's medal as City beat Gornik 2–1. And one of those splendid European nights – a 3–3 draw against Atletico Bilbao in Spain – provided Summerbee with one of his most pleasurable City memories.

'It was a very warm night and the pitch was like a billiard table,' he recalls. 'It started to rain torrentially – straight down, with no wind – which made the surface greasy.

'We were 2–0 down in ten minutes but all of a sudden someone knocked the ball to me, I pushed it past the full-back and he just wasn't there!

'I ripped him to pieces and we drew 3–3, beating them 3–0 in the return. For me, that gave me absolute pleasure, doing exactly what I had been told to do by Malcolm, in terms of how ... how to approach the game and approach the full-back.'

Strangely, Summerbee nominates an altogether more modest setting for his finest ever display in a City shirt – Deepdale, home of Preston North End.

'That Bilbao game gave me a lot of pleasure, but my best game was possibly early in my first season at City, in the second division.

'We won 3–0 at Preston and I gave the full-back the chasing of his lifetime. I don't think he ever touched the ball. Coming from Preston made it that bit special for me.'

Summerbee shared in City's disappointments and near-misses over the coming seasons. The 1972 Championship race, when the Blues won just three of their last eight games to hand Derby the title, stands out. But the exciting winger remained philosophical throughout.

'I honestly never had any disappointments,' he insists. 'I was doing something that I loved doing and count myself privileged to have won anything at all.

'I played because I loved the game, and the more success I got, the bigger thrill the game gave me. If you came to my house today you wouldn't find a medal or a cap. I just count myself lucky to have played at a standard higher than I ever imagined I would and to have won honours that eluded many better players.'

Not even Summerbee's scant number of international appearances ruffles him. 'I was a winger in an era when they didn't have them,' he states simply.

Eight caps spread over five years is small reward for such talent, although he insists: 'It didn't matter whether I got one cap, eight or 80. It's still lovely to play for your country.

Last season . . . Mike (front row second from left) at the start of 1974–75, his last at City. The line-up (back row left to right) Book, Donnachie, Clarke, Booth, MacRae, Oakes, Barrett, Horswill, MacFarlane. (front row) Doyle, Summerbee, Bell, Marsh, Hartford, Tueart, Henson.

'I was on stand-by for the 1970 World Cup in Mexico and I think I could have done quite well there, but Alf Ramsey didn't! And I still think he was as good as you could get as an England manager.'

Summerbee's last international appearance was as a substitute for future City striker Mick Channon in a 2–1 win over the Soviet Union in Moscow in June '73. Four days earlier, Mike endured one of the most frustrating afternoons of his England career, watching his country lose 2–0 to Poland in Chorzow – a defeat that cost England qualification for the 1974 World Cup.

'The game was screaming out to bring wingers on and I said to Alf, just give me 20 minutes against that full-back. I would have loved to have come on, but Alf didn't believe in wingers and wouldn't do it.'

While Summerbee could accept disappointments on the pitch, events off the pitch at Maine Road frustrated him – noticeably the departure of Mercer in 1972.

'I thought Joe was treated very shabbily and I was a bit disappointed in Malcolm at the time,' he reveals. 'I think he was influenced by people on the outside. If it had not been for that, the two of them would probably have stayed together at City for another ten years!

'Gradually, the team started breaking up. Players like Ian Bowyer, Stan Bowles, Colin Barrett were allowed to leave because they weren't accepted by the fans.

'Some older players left when I felt they could have slipped into the reserves and helped the younger lads along.' The final straw for Summerbee was the arrival of Ron Saunders as manager in December 1973. It would be another 15 months before Summerbee left Maine Road for Burnley, but the arrival of Saunders marked the true beginning of the end for the winger.

'He was just not the right man for the particular players we had. He treated us like babies, not the experienced pros we were,' says Mike.

'City wasn't like any other club at the time – there were too many characters and too many good players, and Ron wanted to be the sergeant-major. If he had settled for being a corporal, he might have got away with it!

'We got to the League Cup Final with him in 1974, but our preparation wasn't particularly good; there was a lot of animosity around the place and we lost to Wolves, a game we should really have won.'

Leeds manager Don Revie had wanted Summerbee, but Saunders put a block on the move, leaving him to play one more key part in Manchester football folklore. In the final game of the season, he was part of the City team that won 1–0 at Old Trafford to ensure United were relegated.

'It was a shock to me that we ever scored in that game,' he says. 'I don't think we were that bothered whether or not it was a draw, which would have given United a chance of staying up.

'There was no way we were going to lose but Denis Law just stuck his boot out at a ball and back-heeled it in! I don't think any of us apart from Denis really appreciated what the consequences were. Derby wins always gave me great pleasure, but not that one.

'You don't like putting fellow pros down, especially if they're from the same city.'

In June 1975, this colourful City career was over. Summerbee transferred to Burnley for £25,000 as Tony Book looked to rebuild the Blues.

'I had 18 brilliant months at Burnley,' says Summerbee, com- pleting the story of his playing career. 'Then a brief spell at Blackpool which was a bit of a farce, and two enjoyable years at Stockport.

'They got rid of the manager while I was there and Freddie Pye, the chairman, asked me to step in as player-manager. I did OK and enjoyed it but I had business interests growing and just didn't have the time.'

Summerbee has been working on that business – the produc- tion of luxury shirts – for nearly a quarter of a century. One of his more unusual football exploits drummed up some well-known customers.

After Summerbee's retirement, his old England pal Bobby Moore enlisted him as an extra in the soccer film 'Escape to Victory'. Filming in Budapest, the former City winger teamed up with Pele, Michael Caine, Sylvester Stallone and a cast of hun- dreds to lead a team of Allied POWs to victory over Germany!

It was a great experience, very enjoyable, and I became good friends with Michael and Sly,' says Summerbee. 'I still make shirts for them and stayed with Michael in Hollywood to watch "Rocky" being filmed.'

Summerbee's connections with City grew increasingly tenuous over the following years until his fellow Maine Road great Fran- cis Lee launched his spectacular takeover bid – a bid that Summerbee was only too glad to endorse.

Mike says: 'It needed somebody like Francis to come along and do what he did, people had been looking for a change at the club for perhaps the last ten years. And you can never under-estimate the part those fans played in getting Francis and his consortium around the negotiating table with the old chairman Peter Swales.

'The club has always had such a terrific support and those fans have long memories. They had never forgotten Franny or what a winner he was. Having been starved of success for so long, they threw themselves wholeheartedly behind him.

'The change at the club in just a few short months was incred- ible. Of course, there are no guarantees in football, but if anyone can bring success to the club, he can. Franny has succeeded in everything he has ever done in life. He has the Midas touch but he's also had to work incredibly hard to get to that stage. He puts in 24 hours a day at whatever he's doing and always has done.'

Apart from the return of his old sparring partner, Summerbee was presented with another reason to start going back to his former club in the summer of 1994. The flag for the third generation of Summerbees in the Football League is currently being carried by Mike's son Nicky, who followed his dad's trail by moving to Maine Road from Swindon Town.

'I had no reservations at all about Nick coming to City,' says his proud dad. 'I've kept out of his way throughout his career as much as possible. Everything he's done, he's done on his own and I'm sure he has the ability to be a success at Manchester City.

'Sure, the surname is unusual so everybody knows straight-away who his father is, but I don't think that adds any pressure to what he's doing. He started at Swindon where I had been a player, so he's been through all this before. As I say, he's on his own, but I know if he needs to talk to me, he will do.'

If Summerbee junior does need any advice, Mike would probably just repeat the football philosophy handed to him by the man who helped him become one of the greatest of City Greats.

'Joe Mercer always said "play with a smile",' says Mike. 'That was his philosophy and mine. The boss enjoyed his football, it was his life.

'He also stressed, play every game as if it's your last because your career is so short. That's why you rarely saw Manchester City players missing games through injury.

'He was such a nice man, a humble man with time for everybody. Incredible when you think of what a great player he had been, what he had achieved.

'Only occasionally would he blow his top and get stuck in. I remember losing to Coventry 3–0 one day. Joe had made a tactical mistake, but we should still have murdered them.

'He came into the dressing room and was about to have a go at us when I said: "You can be quiet as well, it's your fault we got beat!"

'He just said: "You're right. That will do," and walked out. 'That's the kind of man he was.

'Joe's death was terrible, he's very sadly missed – as a manager, a person, and a friend. I was at his funeral and a lot of his old Aston Villa friends were telling me Joe had wanted to sign me from the age of 15.

'I signed for City because of Joe Mercer and the greatest pleasure in my life was wearing the pale blue shirt of Manchester City – it was even better than playing for my country.'

Mike Summerbee
FULL INTERNATIONAL CAPS—8 (1 goal)

(England score given first)
1968:   Scotland (Glasgow) 1–1, Spain (Wembley) 1–0, West Germany (Hanover) 0–1.
1971:   Switzerland (Wembley) 1–1 GOAL.
1972:   West Germany (Berlin) sub 0–0, Wales (Cardiff) 3–0, Northern Ireland (Wembley) 0–1.
1973:   USSR (Moscow) sub 2–1.

MANCHESTER CITY APPEARANCES

League: 355 + 2 sub, 47 goals. F.A. Cup: 34, 11 goals. League Cup: 36, 8 goals. Europe: 16, 1 goal. TOTAL: 441 + 2 sub, 67 goals.

CHAPTER SIX

Colin Bell

It was Boxing Day, 1977, and Colin Bell was about to make a short walk he had made hundreds, if not thousands, of times before over the previous 11 years.

It took him the handful of yards from the Manchester City dressing room, down the players' tunnel and out onto the Maine Road pitch where over 45,000 fans were waiting for the start of the second half of City's first division clash with Newcastle United.

For Bell, arguably the greatest of City's many talented and popular post-war greats, this was no ordinary afternoon.

Just over two years earlier, the tireless midfielder had suffered a crippling knee injury in a triumphant 4–0 League Cup victory over Manchester United, and the intervening 25 months had seen Bell play just four games in an abortive attempted comeback.

Now, he was about to take the field as a half-time substitute for Paul Power, and Maine Road was about to acknowledge its favourite son with one of the most moving receptions the ground has ever seen.

Over a decade later, Bell, who by his own admission does not possess the most dependable of memories, can vividly recall the day and what it meant to him.

'I remember it well,' says Bell. 'As I came down the tunnel I could hear a whisper go right round the ground.

'I knew that reception was for me alone. I was never an emotional player – even after I scored I never showed my feelings – but that afternoon I got a big lump in my throat.

'I've been lucky to win cups and medals and play internationals, but of all my great football memories, that is the one that sticks in my mind.

'The City crowd and I had this thing going together, a mutual

Duty calls . . . Bell and City pal Dennis Tueart boarding a plane for an England European Championships trip in 1974–75.

respect really. And that standing ovation from 40,000 people brought a lump to my throat for the only time in my career.'

Like all good fairytales, this particular episode had a happy ending. The game stood goalless at half-time but, inspired by Bell's presence, if not his footballing contribution, City swamped the Geordies 4–0, with Dennis Tueart grabbing a hat-trick.

'I don't think I touched the ball; it was ten men versus 11,' says Bell with characteristic modesty. 'But the atmosphere got to our team and we ran away with it.'

Sadly, the Bell story would ultimately be denied its happy ending. Although he made a further 26 League appearances for City after the Newcastle comeback, Bell's knee would never recover from the massive damage inflicted on it in that fateful challenge with Martin Buchan.

One of the greatest talents City – or, indeed, England – had ever possessed had at least four top-class seasons cruelly snatched from the end of his career.

Today, Bell is predictably philosophical about the years stripped away from him, although he confesses: 'You always feel hard done by in such situations.

'I was 29 when I took my knock and I could have played another three, four, five years with little difficulty. Keeping fit was never a problem. It was just not meant to be.

'I will always look back and think of extra things I could have achieved. There may have been more medals, more caps, I really don't know.

'But this is a man's game, you expect to take knocks and it could have been a lot worse – it could have happened when I was 22, not 29.'

Yet 15 years after he last kicked a football for City, the Bell legend lives on. His name can still be heard ringing around Maine Road on some match days – a tribute to his inspirational role in the most successful side in the club's history.

That legend began in March 1966 as Joe Mercer, on the verge of leading City to the second division Championship, bought the fresh faced 20-year-old from nearby Bury.

Deadline day had approached and Bell, club skipper at Gigg Lane in spite of his tender years, was coveted by two Lancashire clubs – City and first division strugglers Blackpool.

'City were odds on to come up at the time while Blackpool were in the bottom three and looked likely to come down,' Bell recalls. 'City came in for me at the death and there was no selection to be made after that.

'The only thing that bothered me about the move was the fee Joe paid for me – £45,000. It seemed a lot of money for someone just turned 20. I wonder how players cope today when they've been bought for £2 million!'

Born in the County Durham village of Hesleden, Bell had been rejected after trials with Arsenal and Newcastle United. His beloved Sunderland had not even offered him a trial in spite of some eye-catching performances with the Horden Colliery Welfare junior team at inside-right or right-half.

Eventually, Bury manager Bob Stokoe secured the youngster ahead of Huddersfield Town and, at the age of 17, Bell was a second division regular. By a nice twist of fate, Bell's debut came in February 1964 . . . against Manchester City.

Greats . . . three of City's all-time greats, Bell, Rodney Marsh and Dennis Tueart in October 1974.

'I'll never forget the game, because I scored to put us one up,' says Bell. 'I side-footed the ball in from six yards while City were appealing for offside. All I could think about were the headlines I would get in the next day's papers.

'The City keeper Harry Dowd got injured – these were the days before substitutes, remember – so Harry went up front with his arm in a sling and he was City's most dangerous attacker! The inevitable happened and Harry scored the equaliser, which ruined my debut a bit.'

Bell repeated the debut heroics for City – scoring the first in a 2–1 win at Derby County. Malcolm Allison had taken the City squad to Lilleshall in preparation for the game, while Bell made the short trip from Bury to Maine Road to complete his signing.

'The first person I met when I arrived at the ground was Mike Summerbee,' says Colin. 'He had been left behind to get treatment and he showed me around and introduced me to everybody.

'It was typical Summerbee. He's got time for everybody and has the ability to make everyone feel at ease. He has an incredible personality and it was a nice introduction to the club.'

Bell appeared in the final 11 games of the promotion season, although he admits: 'I was always a slow starter and it took me a while to settle in, though I scored four goals before the end of the season which wasn't bad for me.'

One of those goals came at Rotherham and made promotion a mathematical certainty. It also gave Bell his first taste of bubbly thanks to a typical Allison gesture.

'Malcolm being Malcolm, the champagne was out as soon as we got back to the dressing room. It was the first time I'd tasted the stuff,' he says.

'But the thing I was beginning to realise about this team was how confident everyone was, and those first few matches were a good bedding to prepare me for the first division.'

Like most of his young team-mates, Bell spent that season adapting to the first division. And learning some hard lessons.

'We beat Liverpool at Maine Road early that season, and Tommy Smith crocked me on the halfway line. As a youngster I didn't know what it was all about, though in later years you learned not to get too close to certain players if you could help it!'

Having found their feet, 1967–68 reached its halfway point with Mercer and Allison in charge of potential champions.

Says Bell; 'Malcolm just used to say: 'Go out and score more than the opposition.' That was his idea of a team talk!

'There was nothing defensive about us. We all defended as a team and attacked as a team. Malcolm had this belief that we were a better side than anybody and that transmitted itself to us.

'Everyone remembers the "Ballet on Ice" game against Spurs at Maine Road when we beat them 4–1.

'It was incredibly icy that day but we were knocking the ball around like it was an ordinary surface, which it wasn't, while Spurs were slipping all over the place.

'Another game that sticks in my mind was beating Sheffield United 5–2 at our place earlier that season; Stan Bowles scored a couple for us.

'It seemed as though it was meant to be our season. Every time we crossed the halfway line we expected to score. And when we hit the post, the ball seemed to bounce back to one of us or hit one of them and go in.

Nijinsky . . . Colin flies into action on one of his record 48 international

'We put teams under so much pressure and had that important little bit of luck.'

By May, City had to travel to Tottenham and Newcastle with the title in the balance and Manchester United ready to step in if they faltered.

'For me, there was no problem going to Tottenham, we always did well there, and sure enough we won 3–1 and I scored a couple.

'But the problem was the following week. We never seemed to get anything better than a draw up at Newcastle.'

Whoever wrote this particular script, clearly had Bell in mind for the heroic lead. Aside from the fact that the two bitter Manchester rivals were in contention for the championship on the final day of the season, Bell was returning to his native North-east against a club that had rejected him as a youngster.

'We came in at half-time drawing 2–2 and discovered that United, at home to Sunderland, were losing. Still, it could have gone either way. We weren't to know the way things were going to work out.

'In the end we made sure anyway, winning a fabulous game 4–3. I had a hand in three of the goals so I like to think I did my bit.

'I look at the video of the match and it's incredible to see 45,000 people without any fencing or police and there's not a single pitch invasion until right at the end.

'Mind you, over the years I must have spoken to about 90,000 City fans who claim they were there that day!'

At the age of 22 and weeks away from making his full England debut, Bell was at the peak of his profession.

'It was a terrific feeling for me, to be part of the number one team in football. The glory things are the cups and Wembley appearances, but consistency over a long hard season is what it's all about.

'We came back on the coach, stopping at Wetherby to crack open more champagne. And we all had to give a song – I think I gave them a few lines of "Blaydon Races!" '

Bell was just one of a host of talented stars in that City side, but in one aspect of the game he stood head and shoulders above his team-mates, or any other English player of the time.

Bell's work-rate was phenomenal and Allison handed him a nickname that became famous around the world. The ease and grace with which Bell covered every inch of the park reminded the City coach of 'Nijinsky', the legendary thoroughbred race-horse. Over 20 years later, Bell has a confession to make.

'That name has always stuck in my throat a bit. In fact, I've never been happy with people talking so much about the running part of my game,' he says.

'To be noted as a runner rather than a player with a bit of skill and vision is a little annoying. Admittedly, running was a big part of my game because I could do it – basically because I pushed myself harder than most.

'While there was a game to be won, I would run myself into the ground. I'm afraid it was a fallacy that I had three lungs or whatever; it was just I hated to lose more than most people.'

Bell returned for the start of the '68–69 season having won the first of his 48 England caps in a 3–1 victory over Sweden at Wembley. Eagerly looking forward to helping City defend their title, the season quickly became a nightmare.

'That season was frightening, every game was like a cup tie, everybody was desperate to beat us,' he says. 'We weren't used to that one little bit and, before we knew it, the season was halfway through and we were struggling.

'The worst thing of all was going out in the first round of the European Cup to Fenerbahce.

'It was unfortunate that it was our first experience of Europe and it couldn't have been a bigger tournament. At Maine Road, they kicked us up in the air, picked us up, shook our hands and we accepted it.

'When we went there they kicked lumps out of us, there were firecrackers going off and it was a terrifying experience. At least when we got into Europe in later years we knew what to expect, so the Fenerbahce experience had some compensation.'

While City struggled to recapture their League championship consistency over the following two seasons, they more than made up for it by capturing three major cups.

Surprisingly, the three finals – against Leicester in the F.A. Cup, West Brom in the League Cup and Gornik Zabrze in the European Cup Winners' Cup – were not remembered for particularly good football. But en route to those finals, City turned in some dazzling displays.

'Beating Everton in the '69 F.A. Cup semi-final was a terrific performance,' says Bell. 'They had a tremendous midfield – Alan Ball, Colin Harvey, Howard Kendall – and to overcome them was fantastic.

'The following season we beat Schalke 5–1 at Maine Road in the second leg of the Cup Winners' semi-final. We were a goal down from the game in Germany, but just went back to Malcolm's theme – you're better than the opposition, go out and score more than them.

'At the time, while all this was going on, I don't think you appreciated exactly what you were doing. Nobody was keeping count of medals, you just went on from week to week. It's only when you stop playing that you look back on it all with pride.

'Maine Road was like a magnet for the playing staff in those days. People couldn't get into work quickly enough. For example, we used to play head tennis before training and if you weren't there at least an hour before the start of training, you couldn't get on court for a game.'

On average, those successful years of the late sixties and early seventies saw Bell miss around ten games a season; his all-action

Bell at a 1972 photo call.

uncompromising style was beginning to take its toll.

'I was the type of player who never pulled out of anything, I didn't shirk tackles,' he explains. 'I like to think I was the type of person who would give his all in challenges.

'In 1970 I dislocated my shoulder after falling awkwardly, the next season I missed games with injured ankle ligaments. But as a pro' footballer you can't go through your career without getting a few knocks and bruises – if you do, you're cheating yourself.'

City just missed out on another League title in 1972, with people questioning the wisdom of Allison signing Rodney Marsh late in the season when his team were in the Championship driving seat.

Bell agrees that Marsh's style 'upset the apple cart' and a run of three wins in the last eight matches let Derby sneak in to capture the title.

More disappointments were to follow. By the start of the next season, Mercer had left for Coventry City and Allison would leave the following March. The Allison-Mercer 'dynasty' was beginning to crumble.

'Joe leaving was a sad day for me,' says Bell. 'The thing is, everybody is put on this earth to do something, and Malcolm's skill was coaching.

'He knew football inside out and was the best coach you could ever wish for. But when Joe left and Malcolm became manager, it took him out of that role.

'In the following seasons there were a lot of player and managerial changes; the place just wasn't the same. The same people you had known for six or seven years, the wisecracks you had shared, were disappearing. The atmosphere was a bit strained with a bunch of new faces coming in.'

Johnny Hart briefly held the manager's job, quitting through ill-health, and clearing the way for Ron Saunders to take over. Saunders' five month reign as boss was hardly the most auspicious in the club's history, although he helped the Blues to the 1974 League Cup Final with Wolves.

Says Bell: 'In my career I've played in two games of this kind. One was when England drew with Poland at Wembley and missed qualifying for the '74 World Cup, and Wolves was the other.

'If either of those games had been boxing matches, the opposition would have thrown the towel in. We were 1–0 down to Wolves at half-time but I always felt if we pulled one back we would win.

'I got the equaliser and we were never out of their half after that. Then, late on, a ball was played across our area, Rodney Marsh just got a toe to it and helped it in the direction of John Richards who scored the Wolves winner.'

The disappointment of losing the League Cup was hard for the ultra-competitive Bell to stomach. But even that harrowing experience was nothing compared to the draw with Poland, at the same stadium five months earlier.

Needing a win to take them through to the Finals in West Germany, England dominated every aspect of the game but with Polish keeper Jan Tomaszewski playing the game of his life, could only manage a 1–1 draw.

True blue . . . Bell (front row third from left) lines up between Dennis Tueart and Rodney Marsh at the start of 1975–76. Tragically, less than three months after this photo, injury would wreck his career.

'I think Poland got out of their half twice in the entire game – and scored once,' says Bell, the disappointment still evident in his voice.

'We went 1–0 down after Norman Hunter, a great player, was caught in possession on the halfway line. So the pressure was really on us. Their keeper was said to be a bit suspect in some quarters, but we were never out of their area and he was extraordinary.

'Things were so bad that even when we got a penalty, I was convinced Allan Clarke would miss! He didn't, but we just couldn't get the winner.

'I was a bad loser in League games – it would take me until the Tuesday to get a defeat out of the system – but this stayed with me for a long time.

'You only get a chance once every four years to play in a World Cup, to show what you're made of, and I was just getting myself established in the England team. I thought this was my big chance.'

Bell had been to a World Cup Finals, four years earlier in England's defence of the trophy in Mexico. A borderline choice, Bell played the full game in a 1–0 win over Czechoslovakia, but his other two World Cup appearances were not such pleasant memories.

Says Bell: 'Alf Ramsey used me as a sub twice – against Brazil and West Germany – and each time I got off the bench, we conceded a goal! That's the one thing I remember about that World Cup.

'We had a really good team – Brazil were terrified we would reach the Final, which tells you how much we were feared.'

One of the most telling substitutions in England history came in the quarter-final with West Germany in Leon. Leading 2–0, Ramsey decided to take off Bobby Charlton to save him for the semi. Everyone remembers the outcome, a 3–2 defeat for England. What people tend to forget is the man who substituted him.

'That was me,' says Bell. 'The way things worked out in '70 made not qualifying in '74 all the harder to take.'

Generally, Bell's England career was one he can look back on with great pride. In a total of 48 appearances, he was only on the losing side ten times, and still holds the record for the most caps won by a player while at Maine Road.

'It was hard getting my international career off the ground. I seemed to be injured whenever I was called up in the early days.

'After playing in the first division, playing for my country had always been my greatest dream. No matter how many times I played, I still got a lump in my throat every time the letter with the F.A. stamp dropped through the letter box.'

By 1974–75, when an abysmal away record hindered City's League form, Bell was an automatic name on the England team sheet. His consistency marked him out as one of the League's most dependable performers.

But in the autumn of 1975, Bell suffered the unthinkable – a loss of form.

He recalls: 'It was probably the worst period of my career. I don't know what the reasons were, I was still doing all the usual things, but nothing would come right for me.

'Then, two or three games before we played Man United in the League Cup, I suddenly felt everything had come right. I had gone full circle and couldn't do a thing wrong. I thought: "terrific!" '

Bell was to be denied the chance to unleash his rediscovered form on the rest of the first division. With City leading the League Cup derby 1–0, goalscorer Dennis Tueart knocked a through-ball for Bell to chase into the goalmouth.

'I had three options and picked the wrong one,' says Bell. 'I was waiting for the ball to sit up so I could shoot, but it wouldn't so I dragged the ball inside the player, thinking I would change up a gear and go for goal.

'When I went inside, I got whacked on my weight-bearing leg. If you're not weight-bearing, injuries don't normally happen. But I had my other leg off the ground and the impact bent my knee backwards.

'Within a split second it was like a false knee, full of blood. When it sprung backwards, it burst blood vessels, did the cartilage and ligaments.

'I knew straightaway it was a bad one. My knee ballooned in seconds.'

Bell was not to know it, but the most physically and emotionally painful months of his football life were about to start.

'Being stubborn and a bad loser, I thought it might be a month or two before I was back. What I didn't realise was this was THE injury I was not going to get over,

'All credit to City. They gave me all the time in the world and Freddie Griffiths and Roy Bailey, the physios, put tremendous time and effort in on me. It's thanks to them I can walk today.

'But there were six months when I couldn't walk or put an ounce of weight on the leg. My wife Marie was a tower of strength and had to do everything for me. I just sat there thinking in the back of my mind: "I'm going to get over this!" '

Bell was deluding himself. He returned for four games at the end of '75–76 season, re-injuring himself in the penultimate game of that term – a 3–1 win over Arsenal.

'Time went on and I still wouldn't accept I had to retire,' he explains. 'I kept battling away until the summer of '79 when Malcolm came to see me and said: "Don't you think it's time you called it a day."

'It was over three years since the first injury, it wasn't getting any better, and the possibility of retirement was starting to sink in a bit. I knew it was going to happen after all the pain and effort I'd put in. It would have been a lot harder to handle if I had been forced to quit after the first injury.'

Bell ran a successful restaurant in Whitefield before returning to Maine Road in the early 1990s to play an important role on City's coaching staff. Not surprisingly, he is still plagued by questions about that night in November '75.

With typical dignity, he answers them.

'People ask me if I think Martin Buchan meant it – I say, I hope not. He is the only one who would know; I prefer not to know. I'd like to think at that level, a player wouldn't do that on purpose. And, after all, it's a man's game.

'Do I begrudge today's players the money they get? I would rather have played for the money I was paid, with and against the players of my day, than be playing now.

'Do I feel bitter about the way things worked out? Why should I? I picked up a lot of trophies and caps and have a lot of good memories and good friends from football.

'I would never trade them for anything.'

Colin Bell
FULL INTERNATIONAL CAPS – 48
(9 goals)

(England score given first)

1968: Sweden (Wembley) 3–1, West Germany (Hanover) 0–1, Bulgaria (Wembley) 1–1.

1969: France (Wembley) 5–0, Wales (Wembley) 2–1, Uruguay (Montevideo) 2–1, Brazil (Rio) 1–2 GOAL, Holland (Amsterdam) 1–0 GOAL, Portugal (Wembley) 1–0.

1970: Holland (Wembley) 0–0, Northern Ireland (Wembley) sub 3–1, Brazil (Guadalajara) sub 0–1, Czechoslovakia (Guadalajara) 1–0, West Germany (Leon) sub 2–3.

1971: Greece (Athens) 2–0.

1972: West Germany (Wembley) 1–3, West Germany (Berlin) 0–0, Wales (Cardiff) 3–0 GOAL, Northern Ireland (Wembley)

0–1, Scotland (Glasgow) 1–0, Yugoslavia (Wembley) 1–1, Wales (Cardiff) 1–0 GOAL.

1973: Wales (Wembley) 1–1, Scotland (Glasgow) 5–0, Northern Ireland (Anfield) 2–1, Wales (Wembley) 3–0, Scotland (Wembley) 1–0, Czechoslovakia (Prague) 1–1, Poland (Chorzow) 0–2, Austria (Wembley) 7–0 GOAL, Poland (Wembley) 1–1, Italy (Wembley) 0–1.

1974: Wales (Cardiff) 2–0, Northern Ireland (Wembley) 1–0, Scotland (Glasgow) 0–2, Argentina (Wembley) 2–2, East Germany (Leipzig) 1–1, Bulgaria (Sofia) 1–0, Yugoslavia (Belgrade) 2–2, Czechoslovakia (Wembley) 3–0 TWO GOALS, Portugal (Wembley) 0–0.

1975: West Germany (Wembley) 2–0 GOAL, Cyprus (Wembley) 5–0, Cyprus (Limassol) 1–0, Northern Ireland (Belfast) 0–0, Scotland (Wembley) 5–1 GOAL, Switzerland (Basle) 2–1, Czechoslovakia (Bratislava) 1–2.

MANCHESTER CITY APPEARANCES

League: 393 + 1 sub, 117 goals. F.A. Cup: 33, 9 goals. League Cup: 40, 18 goals. Europe: 23, 8 goals. TOTAL: 489 + 1 sub, 152 goals.

CHAPTER SEVEN

Tony Book

The summer of 1966 saw Manchester City preparing for their return to the first division after a three-year absence.

It was during one of the pre-season training sessions that Colin Bell, an exciting young signing from neighbouring Bury, noticed a 'mature' looking footballer jogging around the surrounding track.

Bell recalls: 'I remember seeing this old bloke running around and wondering to myself, "Why have we bought this old codger?" '

The future England star was not alone in his scepticism over this particular Allison-Mercer signing. But 28 years, over 300 City appearances, and numerous honours later, that 'old codger' is still playing an important role at Maine Road.

Tony Book, City's reliable captain throughout the greatest years in the club's history, had not kicked a ball in the Football League until a month before his 30th birthday. But how he made up for lost time.

Certainly Bell and his team-mates did not take long to be convinced that the £17,500 the Blues paid Plymouth Argyle for the former bricklayer was money wisely invested.

'Tony was 31 and classed as coming to the end of his career, yet he had just been bought to play in the first division,' says Bell, explaining the incredulity which greeted Book's arrival at Maine Road.

'I don't know whether it was all good judgement or good luck on Malcolm's part, but Tony was a pearler of a buy.'

It was not only as a talented and athletic right-back that Book would prove his value to the club. After illness forced Johnny Hart to leave the manager's chair in the autumn of 1973, Book became caretaker boss. And after Ron Saunders' ill-fated sojourn

The boss . . . Tony Book with his 1978–79 City squad. The side would finish a disappointing 15th after placing fourth and second in the previous two seasons.

in charge at Maine Road, Book took over on a permanent basis later that season.

Under his command, City enjoyed their most successful period since those halcyon days of the late sixties and early seventies.

And even though Book's reign in charge at Maine Road ended on an unhappy note, 1994 saw him notch up the 28th anniversary of his arrival at City as a key member of Brian Horton's back-room staff.

Book's association with City began at an appropriate venue considering the success he would help bring to Maine Road in the coming years – Wembley Stadium.

'I met Joe Mercer in London and he took me to see the first game of the 1966 World Cup, England v Uruguay,' says Book.

'He invited me up to Manchester where we had further chats and I eventually signed. Leicester were supposed to be showing a lot of interest, but I didn't need a second invitation to join Joe and Malcolm.'

Allison had given Book his chance in League Football at the age of 29. Taking him from the life of bricklayer and part-time footballer with Bath City to second division Plymouth Argyle, where he was manager.

And Allison it was, two years later, who was faced with the task of convincing Mercer that a 31-year-old full-back, with limited League experience, could do an adequate job in the first division.

Allison's tactics, explains Book, were very simple: 'He sold the idea to Joe on the basis that Joe himself had gone to Arsenal from Everton at the age of 32 and enjoyed great success.

'I don't think he needed much convincing after that, although there was obviously that element of chance involved, considering I was nearly 32 and had spent so much time in nonleague.'

Book had flirted with the professional game while at Southern League Bath. He had trials with Nottingham Forest, local side Bristol Rovers had taken an interest, and during National Service days in the early 1950s, Book had turned out for Chelsea reserves.

But the days of the maximum wage for League players meant Book was more financially secure playing part-time. That was until Allison's silver tongue convinced him to try his luck with Plymouth in 1964.

Two years later, Book's rags to riches story went a step further when he was thrust into the first division limelight.

'Obviously, playing first division football was something I had always wanted to do and I was like a kid going into football for the first time,' he recalls.

'But I wasn't overawed by it. The nice thing was there were a lot of young homegrown players at City such as Glyn Pardoe, Alan Oakes, Mike Doyle, and I think they looked up to me because of my age.

'It was amazing really, because I had so little experience, but they appreciated where I had come from and what I had been through to get there.'

Book's debut quickly dispelled any worries that he would be out of his depth in the top flight. It came in a 1–1 draw at Southampton and Book soon learned that age didn't exempt him from practical jokes.

He says: 'I was marking John Sydenham who had been a good left-winger over the years, and I happened to have a useful game.

'We were coming back on the train and Johnny Crossan, our captain, was congratulating me. He told me the local paper had

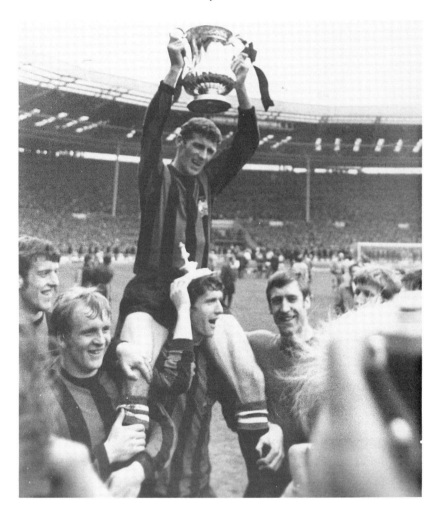

Victorious . . . Book chaired by defender Mike Doyle, with the 1969 F.A. Cup.

a "Monday's Man" award for the man-of-the-match and that I would win it.

'He also told me there was a £500 prize that went along with it. As you can imagine, I was delighted. It took ages for me to realise the story about the money had been a wind-up!'

City's next match brought Liverpool to Manchester, and gave Book an early taste of the sort of fabulous Maine Road games to come.

'There were 50,000 people there and I had never experienced anything like it. I had another tough opponent, Peter Thompson, but we managed to win 2–1.

'For me, that was the beauty of the game in those days. It was very much a game of man-to-man confrontation. Fullbacks knew their job was to mark wingers and I soon learned every week brought a class player and you had to prove yourself against him.'

Book, a natural inside-forward, had been converted to full-back during his Army days and his first season with the Blues often saw him used as sweeper in a five-man defence.

That formation changed in an F.A. Cup quarter-final at Leeds. 'We were very unlucky to lose,' says Book. 'Jack Charlton scored with a late header.

'But that game, and the switch from a five-man to four-man defence made us think we might be capable of doing something.'

That was a huge understatement. A year after his arrival at Maine Road, Crossan left for Middlesbrough, and Book found himself captain of a side that would win the 1968 Championship.

'What a team that was,' he says. 'For me it was brilliant to have somebody like Mike Summerbee outside me.

'He never wanted you to do anything spectacular to put him in. Unlike some wingers he didn't need great passes over defenders; all he asked was that you got the ball to him. Inside, Colin Bell was phenomenal, a great help. If you were ever in trouble, he was always there as a get-out.

'As a team, we complemented each other. Myself and Mike down the right, the "country cousins" of Pardoe and Oakes, and a great thing between Neil Young and Tony Coleman.'

As with other members of the Championship side featured in this book, the 'Ballet on Ice' – the 4–1 destruction of Spurs at an ice-bound Maine Road in early December – and the Championship clincher at Newcastle are games that stand out.

But Book recalls two other special matches during that triumphant campaign.

'I particularly remember beating Everton 2–0 at home near the end of the season, because I got our first goal.

'We hadn't played particularly well and we were just hanging in there when I scored. The reason I remember it so clearly was that the goal was with my left foot, my standing foot!

'The ball dropped nicely outside the box and I just hit it. I didn't

Success . . . Book the manager with the '76 League Cup, along with match winner Dennis Tueart and former chairman Peter Swales.

get that many goals during my career, though I took penalties for a bit before Franny Lee arrived.

'Another important win came at Old Trafford in late March. United were up there with us, but we hammered them 3–1 and that's when we began to think we might be Championship material.'

The deciding game – that incredible 4–3 victory at Newcastle – stands alone as Book's over-riding City memory. As does the thought that flashed through his mind as he realised he was captain of the best side in England.

'Quite simply, I remember thinking: "I never want to go back to bricklaying!" It was a fairytale for me, as simple as that.'

Unfortunately, Book had little time to rest on his laurels. The ensuing pre-season saw him stricken by a career-threatening achilles tendon injury that kept him out of the first 25 games of 1968–69.

'It was the lowpoint of my playing career,' he says. 'We tried everything to get it right, I had it in plaster, had cortisone injections, cortisone tablets, even deep ray treatment.

'If I had been younger they would have operated but because of my age the attitude was, wait and see what happens. I could have been out to grass.'

Book wasn't helped by a premature comeback in the reserves that set him back weeks. In December he made a successful return in a friendly at North-east non-leaguers Crook Town.

By late January, Book was fit enough to take his place in a fourth round F.A. Cup draw at Newcastle. And the Book fairy-tale was about to have another implausible chapter added to it.

'That season, everyone was lifting their game against us in the League. We were knocked out of the European Cup in the first round, but were going well in the F.A. Cup.

'We had some tough draws, including Newcastle and Spurs, but managed to get to the semi-final against Everton at Villa Park.

'I remember going for a walk around Birmingham on the night before the game with Dave Ewing, our trainer.

'Dave knew all about these big games having played for City in the fifties, and he just turned to me and said, "Get a pint down you, it'll help you sleep."

'So we had a couple of drinks and that did the trick. I was never a big drinker but I had a great night's sleep. Mind you, it didn't stop the nerves altogether.'

Young centre-half Tommy Booth ensured Book's nerves survived, scoring a late goal. With Dave Connor doing a special marking job on danger-man Alan Ball, City reached Wembley.

There, Neil Young's winner sank Leicester, and Book's remarkable comeback was capped when he mounted the Wembley steps to accept the F.A. Cup.

That season had another surprise in store for Book. Barely months after injury had cast a shadow over his career, the 34-year-old was named joint Footballer-of-the-Year with Derby's Dave Mackay.

'It was a genuine surprise to me,' he says modestly. 'I only played 15 League games, but I think they must have taken the previous Championship season into account.

'I had been an ever-present that year and felt I might have had

Book, the manager, showing the intensity involved in managing one of football's biggest clubs.

a chance of the award. But United won the European Cup and George Best had to win it.

'It was a tremendous honour, especially sharing it with a man who is one of the all-time greats in my view. To come out of non-league and to have all this happen was incredible. But it was really a recognition of everyone at Manchester City, not just me.'

In spite of his late arrival in the first division and dreadful injury problem, Book had become one of the key elements in the chemistry that made City such a happy and successful club. Any doubts over his age or fitness had long been forgotten – at Maine Road at least.

Says Tony: 'After a while, the age thing was never mentioned.

'I only got stick from opposition players and managers. That was the thing I heard from the touchline – "Take the old so and so on."

'That never bothered me. One of my strengths was pace and I was always pleased when wingers tried to beat me because I knew I had a chance.

'I don't carry any weight and, though I've always enjoyed the odd cigarette, I always wanted to put the training in.

'Joe's attitude was that I should save myself in training and be ready for the Saturday. Malcolm went the other way; he was a fitness fanatic and wanted me to do as much as the rest. In the end, I did my own thing, just what I felt was necessary.'

The following 1969–70 season found City further enhance their reputation as cup kings. But, for Book, the real goal was another Championship.

'Consistency was a difficult thing for us to find over those seasons,' he admits. 'If you look at our cup record, our lack of it was surprising, considering the side we had.

'I think for a while we got carried away by the cup situations. They took precedence which was always a disappointment to me because I always judged my teams on League records.'

It was hardly depression time at Maine Road, however. The European Cup Winners' Cup and League Cup both ended up in Book's hands in the first half of 1970. The latter was a particularly sweet success, involving a two-legged semi-final win over Manchester United.

'They were great games, I think nearly 120,000 people saw the two. We won 4–3 on aggregate, we had the voodoo sign over United in those days.

'There were some classic derbies and they were all the more memorable for me because I always found myself marking George Best.

'Of all the players I've played against, he's the best. No question. You talk about players doing certain things, but he could do the lot.

'I used to run alongside Bestie and say, "Go on. pass the ball." You knew if he didn't have it, you had a chance. If he started getting at you, you had problems.

'Once, at Old Trafford, I misjudged a through ball and he went past me and stuck it in. But I don't really remember him giving me the runaround too often. Mind you, he put that right by sticking six past my brother Kim in an F.A. Cup tie when Kim was in goal for Northampton!'

Best and United had an unfortunate part to play in City's drop in fortunes in 1970–71. In a sad precursor of the injury that would end Colin Bell's career, Best's challenge on fullback Glyn Pardoe broke the City player's leg.

Says Book: 'It was so bad, Glyn could have lost his leg if the doctors hadn't acted quickly.

'His loss was a great one. He was a brilliant left-back, a real unsung hero, and his absence had a lot to do with us going off the boil that season.

'There was a lot of ill-feeling over Bestie's challenge. Malcolm and Joe banned us all from talking to the press about it, but I went to see Glyn in hospital the next day and he didn't bear any malice – that's the sort of lad he was.'

With City's European Cup Winners' defence also ruined by key injuries, the Blues ended a season empty-handed for the first time in three years. Yet in spite of surprisingly mediocre cup displays in '71–72, City and Book came so close to winning another Championship.

That narrow failure, boardroom unrest, and the departure of Joe Mercer for Coventry in June 1972, contributed to the beginning of the end for City's most successful ever side.

'It's never good for a football club when there are things going on in the boardroom,' admits Book. 'And Joe leaving was a great loss for me.

'I had a lot of respect for him as a man. He knew football inside out and knew the way to treat players. He was there when things weren't going right, or if you needed help.

'Although Malcolm had given me my break, we were never that close away from football. The first time he was at the club, I think he was the best coach this country has ever produced. While we had a great working relationship, you would not particularly call it a friendship.

'By the end of the '72–73 season things had gone a bit sour and Malcolm's departure was inevitable.'

Book played in four of City's first nine League games of 1973–74, but when illness forced Johnny Hart to quit as manager after only six months in charge, he was named caretaker boss by new chairman Peter Swales.

'I felt I was ready to manage the club and had a couple of months in charge,' Tony explains. 'I had the respect of the players, I knew they felt I could do it.

'But you don't expect the boardroom to go along with player power and when Ron Saunders was appointed, he asked me to be his assistant. I had decided to go into management and this seemed a great way to start.'

First, however, Book, aged 39, made a decision he still regrets to this day.

'Ron said he thought I should stop playing and I went along with him. I should really have told him I could have been more use on the pitch. I could have seen out that season, but having left myself out when I was caretaker, I didn't really have a leg to stand on.'

Book admits Saunders' reign was not an easy one for anyone concerned. An unhappy club and a League Cup Final defeat by Wolves were its only legacies by the time Saunders was sacked after a 3–0 defeat by QPR in March '74.

Book, now permanent boss, was left to lead City out of relegation trouble late in the season.

'We managed it with a couple of late wins,' he recalls.

'I didn't find it difficult adjusting to management. I had decided to do things my own way and, in spite of having been so close to the lads on the park, they respected the fact it was a different ball game.'

The following summer present the new manager with problems of a different nature as he lost two of his big-name former team-mates, Rodney Marsh and Francis Lee.

'As often happens, Francis came back to haunt us when he went to Derby and scored the goal that effectively won them the title at Maine Road.

'The situation with Rodney was typical of him. I knew what I was dealing with and had to do what I felt was best for the club. Sadly, that meant selling him.'

The replacements Book lined up could hardly be classed as second rate. In a short period came internationals of the calibre

We've done it! . . . Book with the great managerial duo Malcolm Allison and Joe Mercer after winning the 1970 League Cup.

of Joe Royle, Brian Kidd, Dave Watson and 'my best signing', Scottish midfielder Asa Hartford.

After a first full season in which disastrous away form hampered City, 1975–76 brought Book his first managerial triumph.

'Although we only finished eighth, I felt the club was on its way again when we won the League Cup against Newcastle.

'Everyone remembers Dennis Tueart's amazing winner, but the first goal from Peter Barnes gave me as much pleasure. It was a set-piece we had worked on dozens of times in training, but it's so rare those things come off.

'The game I remember particularly well that season was the second leg of the semi-final against Jack Charlton's Middlesbrough at Maine Road.

'We had injuries and suspensions and had to put kids like Kenny Clements, Paul Power and Ged Keegan in. But we got an early goal from Keegan and hammered them 4–0. It was a great night and a tremendous feeling to be going back to Wembley.

'I was also the first man to win the League Cup as a player and a manager which was a nice honour.'

Two events beyond Book's control were to prevent City recapturing the glory days of the previous decade. The first was the cruel career-ending injury to Colin Bell. The second, the departure of right-hand man Ian MacFarlane.

'Ian was a completely different kettle of fish to me and we had a great working relationship going,' says Book. 'I had played with him at Bath and while I was an introvert, he was outgoing and got the best out of the players on the training pitch.

'It was sad but one of those unavoidable things when he left, over an argument whether or not the club should buy his house up in Middlesbrough where he had come from.'

Early the following season, Book made his biggest mistake in management as he sought to make up for the traumatic loss of Bell.

'I wanted to buy Alan Ball from Arsenal, but I got outvoted at boardroom level. It was the biggest boob I ever made; I should have stuck to my guns.

'We were constantly looking for Colin's replacement, trying all sorts of things, but of course we never found the answer.

'With Colin in the side, or if we had got Alan Ball, we would have won the League in '77. No danger.'

A runners-up place to Liverpool was hardly a disgraceful performance, but Book is still haunted by that season.

'You talk about how things turn on you in football, well we came within one game of winning the League,' says Book.

'We played Liverpool at home in December when it was incredibly icy. And we were leading 1–0 until Dave Watson headed an own goal with two minutes left. You could never come closer to winning it than that.'

The much-respected Bill Taylor had replaced MacFarlane, although his similarity to Book meant the partnership never succeeded in the same way. And the summer of '77 saw Book make one of his few ineffective signings – Mick Channon.

'Even though there were a few of these little disappointments, it was still a great time for us,' insists Book. 'We had replaced the old favourites and I took City into Europe three times running, so there wasn't too much wrong.'

Still, Book sought Bell's replacement. In the summer of '78 a move for Gerry Francis collapsed on the medical and Middlesbrough's Graeme Souness committed himself to Liverpool.

By January 1979, City decided the answer was to bring back Malcolm Allison. For Book, still fiercely loyal to the club, it is a difficult subject to discuss, even years later.

'I found myself in a difficult situation,' he admits. 'In spite of our success, Malcolm wanted to change things around completely and go with younger players. Wherever Malcolm has gone, he has always liked to build his own teams.

'That wasn't for me. That's not to say the likes of Ray Ranson, Nicky Reid, Tommy Caton or Michael Robinson wouldn't have been decent players for City if they had been given time, but they were rushed into it.

'It was the worst period I've gone through at the club. Very difficult. But things were taken out of my hands.'

Apart from a UEFA Cup quarter-final appearance against Borussia Monchengladbach in '79, the following season-and-a-half was a traumatic time for Book, City and their fans. Finally, in October 1980, he was put out of his misery.

'I was basically an assistant manager by the time we were dismissed and, although our sacking was inevitable, it was still the lowpoint of my City career,' he says.

Book describes his belated football stardom as a 'fairytale' and, true to the script, even this low period had a happy conclusion.

He spent six months working at Cardiff City in an advisory capacity and, as a former F.A. Cup winning captain found himself invited to City's Centenary Final appearance against Tottenham in 1981.

'I couldn't believe the reception I got that day,' says Book, still clearly moved by the response which greeted his introduction before the Final.

'I had a lot to do with supporters' clubs when I was manager and I always knew this club and its fans were a bit special.

'So, when John Bond offered me a job on the youth development side, I remembered that reception and realised I had to come back.'

Since then, Book has held a number of vital backroom jobs at Maine Road, working with the highly successful youth sides, reserves, and with first teamers on the training pitch. He was even called in as caretaker again, after the sacking of Mel Machin in 1989 and Peter Reid four years later.

'A jack-of-all-trades,' is how he modestly described himself. City fans, as loyal as Book himself, would say otherwise.

'I suppose, for the good of my career, I should have left City when Malcolm came back. But things haven't worked out badly,' he says.

'I love the place. I love everything involved with the management and staff at Maine Road, and no-one will ever take that away. The people I've worked with and under have been absolutely first-class, and that's what binds you to the place.'

Tony Book
MANCHESTER CITY APPEARANCES

League: 242 + 2 sub, 4 goals. F.A. Cup: 28, 0 goals. League Cup: 19, 1 goal. Europe: 17, 0 goals. TOTAL: 306 + 2 sub, 5 goals.

CHAPTER EIGHT

Joe Corrigan

The story of Manchester City's giant keeper Joe Corrigan is a story of triumph over adversity; a story of a man forced to endure the cruellest personal and professional abuse; but, ultimately, the story of a man who succeeded through sheer determination and effort.

That story took Corrigan from the depths of ridicule, and saw him transformed into a fitting successor to the tradition of brilliant City number ones.

For many difficult seasons, the legacy of Frank Swift and Bert Trautmann was a millstone around Corrigan's young neck. Eventually, he would graduate to international status and be justifiably talked about in the same breath as those great keepers.

The man himself vividly remembers one game that marked a turning point in his troubled career.

It was March 1975, and Keith MacRae, the promising young Scotsman bought to replace Corrigan, had been injured in a defeat at Leicester. Corrigan had been brought back for one last chance.

Big Joe takes up the story: 'I came back in a game at QPR and things seemed to go really well from there.

'There was one point in one match that particularly stands out. We were playing Wolves and I went up for a cross and got really floored by Derek Dougan.

'John Richards put the rebound in, but luckily the referee disallowed it. In the bad old days, that goal would probably have stood and everyone would have blamed me. Even though we lost 1–0 that day, things seemed to go really well from then on.'

The 6ft 4½ in keeper appeared in 217 of City's next 218 League games, won England caps, a League Cup winner's medal, an F.A. Cup loser's medal and, perhaps most significantly of all, three player-of-the-year awards from the same supporters who had spent so many seasons making his life a misery.

Corrigan's remarkable rise to the pinnacle of his profession was aptly summed up in a perfect setting – Wembley, and the 100th F.A. Cup Final.

History shows that Tommy Hutchison's freak own goal denied City victory. The 1–1 draw handed Tottenham a chance they scarcely deserved to replay and win the cup 3–2. History also shows that Corrigan was twice made man-of-the-match after performances that showed a worldwide TV audience he was worthy of playing a greater role in an England set-up dominated by Peter Shilton and Ray Clemence.

The Centenary Cup Final defeat remains a disappointment to Corrigan. 'We lost the game on the Saturday,' says Joe. 'I'm sure Glenn Hoddle's free-kick was going wide until Tommy got in the way and deflected it past me.

'For me, the F.A. Cup Final is all about the Saturday. The players are all hyped up, the fans are all hyped up, the TV is all hyped up. The Cup Final is meant to be all about who is best on the day.

'I've no doubt that on the Saturday, we were the better team. If we followed the example of American football and had sudden-death in extra-time, I'm sure we would have won.

'The second game did not feel like an F.A. Cup Final. It was just like another League match and, with all the Spurs fans there, we might as well have been playing at White Hart Lane.'

Nevertheless, Corrigan had come a long way since the days of the late sixties and early seventies when a promising career seemed to be heading nowhere.

A moment that everyone remembers from this difficult period came in an horrendous 5–1 home defeat by West Ham in March 1970. Of the five goals put past Corrigan, one has been replayed hundreds of times.

Corrigan, jogging back to his line after making a goal kick, watches in disbelief as West Ham's Ronnie Boyce volleys the ball first time into an open goal from just inside the City half!

'I must have a word with the BBC about royalties, the number of times they've shown that goal. It's been on more often than some adverts,' jokes Corrigan.

'I remember it vividly. Ronnie's volley could have gone anywhere, and no-one would have remembered it. But at least I learned a lesson, which is what goalkeeping is all about. From then on, I never turned my back after making goal kicks!'

If that was one lowpoint, things would get worse before they improved. Corrigan possibly hit the real depths in 1973–74.

'It was a funny period all round with changes in management and a lot of players getting old,' he says.

'I'm not saying I was blameless, obviously I wasn't, but things had begun to fall apart when we bought Rodney Marsh in March '72. We were clear at the top of the table and beat Chelsea in Rodney's first game. But I slipped a disc and we only won three of our last eight games, finishing fourth.

'In spite of his obvious ability, Rodney wasn't the influence he had been expected to be. Malcolm Allison went, other players went and the whole club was going through a transitional stage – I was just part of that.'

The common criticism levelled at Corrigan throughout the disappointing years of the early seventies concerned his weight. It's a criticism to which the giant keeper still objects.

'Everybody talked about weight problems but that was a lot of nonsense. There was no weight problem,' he says. 'But one thing that was a big help happened just before Ron Saunders arrived as manager in '73–74.

'I broke my jaw and had it wired up for three weeks. I lost about a stone in that time and felt really fit when I came back. That played a big part in keeping me down to 14–14½ stone, which was my ideal playing weight.'

Weight problem or not, manager Johnny Hart seemed to have signalled the end of Corrigan's City career in October 1973, when he paid a record-equalling £100,000 to Motherwell for MacRae.

'I did go on the transfer list in response to that signing. After all it equalled the record for a goalkeeper back then,' admits Corrigan.

'But I accepted it as part and parcel of the game. You have these situations in football and have to battle away. If you give up, you not only lose the club you are at, you carry a reputation as a quitter with you wherever you go. I was determined to at least go down fighting.'

Man of the match . . . Joe making yet another stunning save on the way to his award in the '81 F.A. Cup Final with Spurs.

Looking back, Corrigan clearly remembers the personal lowpoint of this time at Maine Road. It followed a poor display in a 3–0 defeat in Burnley in late September.

It was common knowledge that City were looking to replace him, but nothing could have prepared Corrigan for the next day's local paper.

He recalls: 'I looked at the back of the paper, and across the top were the pictures of ten goalkeepers under a headline "Which one are City going to buy?"

'I had been slaughtered in that day's papers and, while I know the press lads have a job to do, I could not accept that. I think they delve a little too deep sometimes and forget they are dealing with people with emotions like anyone else.'

Corrigan should have guessed his City career would be far from straightforward. He made his debut as an 18-year-old in a League Cup clash with Blackpool in October 1967.

'The first time I touched the ball it went through my legs!' says Corrigan. 'But I did quite well after that, we drew 1–1 and I kept my place for the replay in which we won 2–0.'

The keeper's very arrival at Maine Road had been out of the ordinary. As a pupil at Sale Grammar School, Corrigan had stopped playing organised football, appearing instead as a second row forward for the school rugby team.

It was while working as an apprentice at AEI that Corrigan appeared as a centre-half in a works game. An impressed colleague asked if the 16-year-old would like a trial at Maine Road and, jokingly, Corrigan said he would.

'City signed me that night, after my first trial,' says Corrigan. 'It was the sort of situation you would never have today. Clubs had more commitment to youngsters in those days. A lot of future first team players came through the youth ranks and saved City a lot of money.'

Signed by Joe Mercer, Corrigan found himself involved with the most successful City squad in the club's history.

'There was such a bubbly atmosphere about the place,' he says. 'The great thing about Malcolm Allison was that he treated every player the same.

'It didn't matter if you were in the first team or the B team. I was only a kid but I could tell Malcolm was a great coach; he was more like another player than management.

'Joe used to be the front man, the ambassador. He was the manager and everyone knew it, and together the pair complemented each other perfectly. Malcolm may have had a terrible name off the field sometimes, but Joe could smooth anything over!'

Still, Corrigan found himself third choice keeper to the ever-reliable Harry Dowd and capable understudy Ken Mulhearn. It took injury to Dowd, and Mulhearn being cuptied, for Corrigan to get a taste of first team football in those League Cup ties. And it took three months away from Maine Road to mark the first big change in Corrigan's career.

Says Corrigan: 'I had three months at Shrewsbury under Harry Gregg. Even though I only played reserve games, I learned so much.

'Harry was tremendous, a man who knows what keeping is all about and who was one of the all-time greats himself. Up until then, my career had been at a stalemate. Within a couple of months of coming back, I made my full League debut.'

The youngster's improvement had been duly noted and earned him appearances against Ipswich, Nottingham Forest, Leeds and Liverpool. The first three matches ended in single goal defeats and Corrigan had to wait until the final games of the season – with Dowd rested for the F.A. Cup Final – for his first clean sheet.

'We beat Liverpool 1–0 at Maine Road and those games gave me the chance to really show what I could do. Luckily, I did OK and the next season, with some pushing from Malcolm, I was first choice.'

Corrigan could hardly have picked a better season in which to establish himself. Winner's medals in the European Cup Winners' and League Cups were topped off by an England under-23 call-up against the Soviet Union.

'Both Finals were tremendous thrills, real Roy of the Rovers stuff,' says Joe. 'The League Cup win over West Brom especially. Here I was, three years after playing Sunday football and school rugby, at Wembley.'

Corrigan didn't get off to the most auspicious of starts. With the Wembley pitch ruined by a combination of snow and the Horse of the Year Show, the sixth minute saw the City keeper fail to field Ray Wilson's cross, and Jeff Astle headed Albion in front.

'That could have been diastrous for me,' admits Joe. 'But I went on to have one of my best games for City.'

Unlikely goalscorers Mike Doyle and Glyn Pardoe guaranteed Corrigan his first winner's medal and City's impressive 2–1 win over Poles Gornik Zabrze in Vienna added a second.

That season also brought the personal thrill of playing for the first time against the Manchester United stars – Best, Law, Charlton – he had watched from the terraces as a young United fan.

Any red allegiances were quickly forgotten as Corrigan kept a clean sheet in front of 63,000 in City's 4–0 Maine Road win.

Corrigan had an unfortunate role to play in City's defence of the European Cup Winners' Cup in 1970–71. He was one of a number of key personnel out for the semi-final second leg against Chelsea at Maine Road.

Absent through injury, his deputy Ron Healey was credited

The City connection . . . Joe with four team-mates and City coach Bill Taylor on England duty in 1976–77. (left to right) Corrigan, Dave Watson, Dennis Tueart, Taylor, Mike Doyle, Joe Royle.

with the own goal that saw City lose their hold on the cup, 1–0 on the night, and 2–0 on aggregate.

'It was such a disappointment to get that close again only to lose, but things were slowly starting to break up at City,' says Joe. 'There were still great players at the club and the club was starting to look for others.

'This was where Malcolm's influence started to come through; his desire to be a manager. He did it all at the wrong time. The team was in a slow decline, but he took the reins and really got too close to the players. He could never be as successful on his own as he had been with Joe.'

City came so close to winning the title the following season, but Corrigan's own decline in form was just a part of the overall backdrop of boardroom and management unrest.

As things worsened, the pressure on Corrigan became increasingly unbearable. He dreaded the thought of playing at Maine Road, had difficulty sleeping and talk of quitting the game was becoming more common. Even today, the affable goalkeeper would be forgiven for viewing those seasons with bitterness.

'I have no bitterness,' he says categorically. 'It's a part of football that will never go away. In fact, I was fortunate because

I think the press were a little kinder in my day. They would lay off a bit; I would hate to go through the same thing now.

'It made success all the sweeter in later years. But my view was that I was paid to do a job to the best of my ability.

'At times that wasn't good enough to get into the first team and I accepted that. It's alright moaning in the press or wherever, but you prove your worth out on the pitch. It's a game where you can't hide – especially in goal!'

With MacRae injured in March '75, City could find no replacement; Corrigan's form soon meant they no longer wanted one. A run of 198 consecutive League games got underway on November 8 1975 with a 2–0 home win over Birmingham. It ran until August 1980.

Aside from the statistics, Corrigan was helping City reestablish themselves at the forefront of the English game. The transfer deadline in March 1975 could have seen Corrigan leave Maine Road. Within a year he had returned to Wembley with City, and within 14 months was an England player!

'I thought that League Cup win over Newcastle in '76 was the start of another great team at City,' says Corrigan. 'Dave Watson proved what a commanding centre-half he was that season. As a keeper, it made such a difference playing behind two great centre-halves like Dave and Mike Doyle at Wembley.

'I just remember the feeling of disbelief after I saw Dennis Tueart's incredible winner go in. Twelve months earlier I had been told I was useless. Here I was, a Wembley winner.

'It just goes to show what you can do if you're prepared to work at it. Something Dennis had said to me when I got back in the first team really stuck with me.

'He pointed out that getting to the top is relatively easy, it's working hard to stay there that's the difficult bit.'

Getting to the top is exactly what Corrigan achieved when, at the age of 27 in May 1976, he was given his England debut.

'Being picked for the squad was incredible,' says Joe. 'Shilton and Phil Parkes dropped out of a tour to the States for the Bicentennial celebrations. I remember sitting back and wondering how on earth people could turn down the chance of playing for their country.

'When I finally made my debut I was lucky that I didn't have long to think about it. The arrangement had been that Ray Clemence would play the first game against Brazil, Jimmy Rimmer would play against Italy and I would come in against the USA.

'But at half-time of the Italy game, Les Cocker the trainer told me to get stripped and come on as a sub for Jimmy. We were 2–0 down at the time and, while I'm not saying I had anything to do with it, we won 3–2!'

Apart from a League Cup winners' medal, 1975–76 brought Corrigan another gratifying honour – the first of his player-of-the-year awards from the City supporters.

'That was one of the sweetest moments I ever had, perhaps even the highlight of my career,' says the keeper who kept 13 clean sheets in 41 League games that term.

'I don't know why that should be. But I had been through all this stick and yet the fans were voting me THEIR player. People talk about cups and internationals, but that meant a hell of a lot to me.'

City never capitalised on Tony Book's excellent work in guiding City to the League Cup in '76.

'As everyone knows, the major factor was the injury to Colin Bell,' explains Joe. 'It was a tragic injury, and the greatest sadness of all was seeing him after he came back.

'He was nicknamed "Nijinsky" but I reckon he could have outrun Nijinsky. He was such a great athlete and allround footballer. He was even a good goalkeeper. He had everything.'

Everything except immunity from injury. Without him, City played entertaining football throughout the 1970s without capturing another trophy. Corrigan himself made two further England appearances in the 1970s – draws with Brazil and Wales – but found further progress hampered by Ron Greenwood's decision to 'platoon' keepers Shilton and Clemence.

Joe has a very definite view of that practice. 'I will always cherish my caps. Playing for my country and being a regular in the squad from '76 to '82 was something they can never take away from me.

'But I do feel, when they decided to rotate Shilts and Ray, they

Wembley heroes . . . Joe celebrates after the '76 League Cup win.

should have rotated the three of us. I have no axe to grind, but Shilts was at Stoke, a relegation team, and had twice pulled out of the set-up.

'City were always at the top and in Europe. For that reason alone, I thought I was worth a bit more international experience. But I accepted that was the manager's decision and I was always ready to play when called upon.'

A trademark of Corrigan's impressive and ever-improving consistency was the gruelling training regime the keeper set himself.

He explains: 'I loved training. My philosophy is, keepers have to be mentally twice as sharp as outfield players. You might have nothing to do for 89 minutes, then win or lose the game with one save.

'I developed techniques from Harry Gregg and Bill Taylor, the City coach, and kept a lot of his routines going when he left. I would work alone after training and even come in on a Saturday morning before the game. After all, you could train Friday in brilliant sunshine and it could be pouring down on the game day. You have to be prepared for every eventuality.'

Back at Maine Road, Malcolm Allison returned in 1979 in an effort to rekindle the former glory days. Allison may have handed Corrigan his start in football, but the keeper did not welcome him back with open arms.

He says frankly: 'I couldn't believe it when he came back. I had a lot of time for Malcolm as a coach but I don't think he could handle senior players. And we had nine internationals in the side at the time.

'He tried to recreate what he had done in the 1960s by bringing kids in. The established stars went and had it not been for the chairman, I would have been on my way too. I agree with giving youngsters a go, but you do it one at a time. We were throwing four or five in at the deep end and getting hammering after hammering.

'Malcolm just had this obsession that they were going to be the saviours of Manchester City.'

As club captain, representing the view of the playing staff, Corrigan also found himself in conflict with the new management.

He explains: 'Hopefully I was doing what I was paid to do on the park but I also had to get involved on the management side. I was the mouthpiece for the players, they told me things and asked me to sort them out, which meant I was always in conflict with Malcolm. It was not a good situation.

'We hit rock-bottom in '79–80, only just escaping relegation and losing to Halifax in the cup. That was the joke at the time – the Americans spent so many millions to get to the moon, City spent £4 million and couldn't get past Halifax!

'The only good thing from a personal point of view was that '79–80 and '80–81 were probably my best seasons. The first year I came fourth in the national sportswriters' player-of-the-year poll. Mind you, I was getting so much practice because we were getting hammered every week!'

When Allison was finally sacked at the start of 1980–81, Corrigan breathed a sigh of relief. 'I could go back to doing what I was paid to do – play football – instead of being at loggerheads with Malcolm.'

Predictably, the City man viewed the arrival of John Bond from Norwich as a godsend.

'John was a brilliant players' manager with different coaching ideas that were more football orientated than Malcolm's, involving more ball work.

'We were unlucky to get knocked out of the League Cup semis – the ref robbed us against Liverpool at Maine Road – and, of course, got to the F.A. Cup Final.

'The following season was a tremendous year, with the signing of Trevor Francis. Unfortunately, he got a lot of injuries and, though we still did very well, we didn't replace people like Gerry Gow and Tommy Hutch who had been such an influence the year before.'

F.A. Cup defeat at Brighton in January 1983, combined with problems off the field, marked the end of Bond's stay at City and, Corrigan realised, his own.

'I knew I was on my way. With the club's financial situation, City couldn't afford to keep the higher-paid players.

'It was very sad to leave but, on reflection, I should really have left when Malcolm came back a second time. People talk about loyalty, but maybe I was too loyal and out-stayed my welcome by four or five years.'

Fittingly, Corrigan was spared the sadness of seeing City relegated at the end of that 82–83 season. By then, he was playing in America, transferred to the Seattle Sounders for £30,000, an experience he thoroughly enjoyed in spite of the League's troubles. Not so happy was a spell at Brighton and a worrying neck injury Corrigan suffered in a reserve game against QPR.

'I had a burst disc that paralysed my left-side temporarily and meant I couldn't do anything for nearly two years,' he reveals.

'I had to have a bone graft on my neck and that's what finally finished me off at the age of 36. There was always the danger that a funny knock in a game could leave me paralysed for life.

'But for that, I could have played on. John Burridge at Newcastle and Shilts at Derby played into their forties. What you lose in reflexes, you make up for in anticipation and experience.'

Corrigan's League career concluded with loan spells at Norwich and Stoke. Both clubs were interested in signing him, but contractual difficulties at Brighton prevented that.

With a nice sense of occasion, the last of Corrigan's 524 Football League games came on Boxing Day 1984. Joe, aged 36, helped Stoke to a rare 2–1 win. It was one of just three games relegated Stoke won that season. It came against Manchester United.

Corrigan is now a specialist freelance goalkeeping coach and for some time Manchester City was a regular port of call. For a self-confessed United fanatic as a kid, Big Joe has found it difficult to leave Maine Road!

'Every club I've worked at as a coach has made me feel welcome and the keepers have been fantastic,' he says.

'I still love Manchester City. People talk a lot about City fans, and their only problem is they are still searching for the success they've had in the past. You can't blame them for that, and in spite of everything that happened to me, no-one will ever convince me they are anything but the best.'

Joe Corrigan
FULL INTERNATIONAL CAPS – 9

(England score given first)
1976: Italy (New York) 3–2.
1978: Brazil (Wembley) 1–1.
1979: Wales (Wembley) 0–0.
1980: Northern Ireland (Wembley) 1–1, Australia (Sydney) 2–1.
1981: Wales (Wembley) 0–0, Scotland (Wembley) 0–1.
1982: Wales (Cardiff) 1–0, Iceland (Reykjavik) 1–1.

MANCHESTER CITY APPEARANCES

League: 476. F.A. Cup: 37. League Cup: 52. Europe: 27. TOTAL: 592.

CHAPTER NINE

Dennis Tueart

The second half of the 1976 League Cup Final was just over a minute old when City's Scottish international left-back Willie Donachie floated a teasing cross deep into the Newcastle United area.

Tommy Booth, a player who might not even have been on the field had it not been for a tragic injury to Colin Bell during the Wembley run, rose and headed the ball back towards the penalty spot.

In the blink of an eye, Dennis Tueart, back to goal, unleashed an overhead kick that had the stunned Newcastle goalkeeper beaten from the moment it left his boot.

It was a goal fit to grace any Wembley occasion, a goal that sealed City's 2–1 victory and a goal that secured Tueart's status as a Maine Road terrace legend.

And for Tueart, proud of his Geordie background, it was a goal that lives strong in his memory over a decade later.

'If you had asked any schoolboy to paint their ideal scenario for a Wembley final, I think this would have been it,' says Tueart.

'To score a spectacular winning goal, in front of 100,000 people, against your home town team, and the team that had rejected you as a kid – it was all extraordinary.

'People still say to me that it was the kind of shot that could have gone anywhere, but I disagree. The truth is I had always been good at volleying, in fact I scored a better goal in the first game of that season against Norwich.

'Tommy Booth was superb in the air, so it was no surprise that his header was so accurate – and a second later I was off on my travels. If Asa Hartford hadn't caught hold of me, I think I'd still be running now!'

The moment was pure Tueart and went some way to explaining

the relationship he had with the City fans still searching for a charismatic hero in the Lee-Summerbee-Marsh mould.

Tueart had arrived at Maine Road just under two years earlier, in March 1974, in a complicated deal that involved Micky Horswill accompanying him from Sunderland and Tony Towers moving to the North-east. Tueart himself was valued at £275,000 and, in spite of some fond memories of his time at Roker Park, Tueart could not move to City quickly enough.

'Things had been falling apart at Sunderland from the previous November,' he says. 'We had won the F.A. Cup in '73 but failed to win promotion because our squad quite simply wasn't big enough.

'We were out of the European Cup Winners' Cup by November and I asked to go on the list, but the club wouldn't sell me in spite of interest from West Ham, Spurs and Derby.

'Eventually I was told that if I came off the list they would let me go before the deadline, the following March.'

The internal politics involving Tueart, a hero at Roker, cup-winning manager Bob Stokoe and the Sunderland board continued until the bitter end. The Sunday before deadline day, Tueart and Horswill – by now also on the list – were told to meet Sunderland officials and be ready for transfer talks.

'They wouldn't give me any information, and I suppose I was a bit naive so I didn't ask,' he says. 'All I knew was that I wanted to be with a club with a bit of ambition. We drove to Wetherby Turnpike and when I discovered it was Manchester City, I was delighted.'

Tueart was met by a high-powered City delegation of Ron Saunders, his assistant Tony Book, chairman Peter Swales and Towers.

'Denis Law is a big hero of mine. And players like Bell, Lee, Marsh, Summerbee were all my kind of players. They believed in my kind of football, open, exciting, enjoyable – that's what excited me about the move,' he recalls.

Derby desperately tried to convince Tueart to join them, but it was only years later that he learned his career could have taken an even more meteoric path.

'I bumped into the Liverpool chief exec Peter Robinson much later and apparently Bill Shankly was furious with Bob Stokoe.

Spot on . . . as City fans remember Dennis the penalty king. Newcastle are on the receiving end in January '75.

He had been promised first refusal when Sunderland sold me.'

Whatever the machinations of his departure, it was sad that Tueart's Sunderland career had to end in such acrimonious circumstances. His role in the '73 Cup Final shock win over Leeds guaranteed him a place in Wearside folklore and Stokoe's insistence that Towers, an England under-23 international of no little ability, move north stemmed from the realisation that the club's supporters would not tolerate Tueart leaving without a 'name' replacement.

His promise had been apparent from his early youth team days, but what had not been quite so apparent was his versatility. A left-winger from an early age. Tueart was a rarity in that he was naturally right-footed.

In years to come, that would make him one of the first division's most feared attackers, capable of turning a defender either way. It also helped extend his City career in later seasons as successive managers switched him to an orthodox striking role and even an attacking midfield position.

On leaving Wearside, Tueart had much to thank Sunderland for. At 15-years-old and barely 5 feet tall, his beloved Newcastle had snubbed him. But the rivals from Wearside had stepped in via their diminutive scout Charlie Ferguson.

'Charlie was about the same size as me and told me it had never stopped him playing,' says Tueart. 'And Sunderland gave me my first sniff of success.

'If my F.A. Cup winner's medal in '73 gave me the thirst, it wasn't until I moved to City and won again at Wembley in '76 that I got the satisfaction. It's like sipping a glass of wine, then being allowed to finish it!'

If Tueart had been longing for the bright lights, the big city action, the pressure and accolades, he did not have to wait long. His debut came on March 13 1974 in a goalless Maine Road draw with Manchester United in front of 51,000. Goal-less the game may have been, devoid of incident it most certainly was not.

'The day didn't get off to the best of starts – I went to the wrong entrance and the doorman, who didn't recognise me, wouldn't let me in because I didn't have a pass,' says Tueart.

'Once the game got underway, I couldn't believe what I was seeing. Big Jim Holton was marking Mike Summerbee – and I mean MARKING – and every time I got the ball Tommy Docherty and Tommy Cavanagh on the United bench were screaming "Break his leg!"

'I later learned this was just a typical derby. There were fights going on all over the place, but no-one was taking them seriously. But eventually Clive Thomas, the referee, had enough.

'He sent Mike Doyle and Lou Macari off, but neither of them would go! They just looked at Clive saying something like: "You can't send us off; this is normal!"

'So Clive took both teams off to cool down and when we came back out, Mike and Lou weren't there.

'It was crazy, but the game itself proved my decision to leave Sunderland was right. This was the sort of quality atmosphere, the real big time, I had been looking for. I'd toyed with it at Sunderland, now I wanted the real McCoy.'

Shortly before leaving the North-east Tueart himself had ended up on the wrong end of a refereeing decision in a derby game, sent-off for the second time in his career in a clash with Middlesbrough.

His indiscretion earned him a three-game ban over Easter 1974 and Tueart, with Saunders' blessing, left training on the eve of

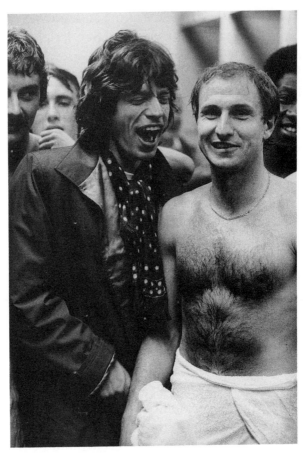

Superstars . . . Dennis and Rolling Stone Mick Jagger, a friend from his days in New York.

Good Friday to spend the holiday weekend in the Northeast. On Good Friday morning, Saunders was sacked.

'Personally, I had never had any problems with Ron, but his handling of some of the other players was scandalous,' says Tueart. 'He had decided certain senior players were of no use to him and just switched himself off to them. That was his biggest downfall.

'Tony Book was his assistant and was appointed manager that afternoon and in my opinion he went on to become the best manager City have had for years.

'He bought very well and had a lot of qualities. Perhaps he was a bit cautious when a bit of flamboyance would have done the job, but gradually he helped us re-establish ourselves.'

The following season, 1974–75, was one of consolidation as City finished a creditable eighth.

'Law, Lee and Summerbee had gone, but Tony bought Asa Hartford and Joe Royle that season. Joe Corrigan was just coming on stream, Doyle was superb at the back and Dave Watson came the following summer.

'Colin Bell was simply brilliant and, the following season, with youngsters like Peter Barnes and Gary Owen coming through, Tony's team really flourished.'

City finished in the same eighth place the following season, but that was more than compensated for by that unforgettable League Cup run. Tricky ties with Norwich and Nottingham Forest were successfully negotiated before the fourth round draw paired City with Manchester United – and presented Tueart with one of his finest hours in a sky blue shirt.

'That game was a high and a low for me,' he remembers. 'A high because of the result and because I had played well; a low for the club because we lost Colin Bell through injury. He was 28 and about to give City the best four years of his career – we never replaced him.'

The game was scarcely 35 seconds old when Tueart grabbed the first City goal in their 4–0 win.

'It was a typical derby. If there is an early goal you know you are in for a cracking game, if not, you know it's going to be a slog.

'That match was the highlight for Book's team, because we were able to flourish and express ourselves against a very good side. Asa got a cracking goal just after the half hour and I added a third just before half-time. It was an unusual match to say the least.

'That result was justified; we were a balanced side who always went forward and aimed to play attractive football. That was part of our problem away from home; we could have done with being a bit more disciplined sometimes and maybe we would have fared better in the League.'

Yet the cost of that 4–0 win over United may never be fully appreciated, as Tueart explains: 'Colin's loss was not only a blow

Match winners . . . Tueart with Peter Barnes, scorer of the first goal, and
bloody hero Dave Watson after the '76 League Cup Final.

to Manchester City, but to the country as well. I would say he
was the most complete footballer I ever saw and his absence cost
us at least one Championship.'

That League Cup run held further drama for Tueart, in addition to the Wembley stunner. A two-legged semi-final date with
another North-east side, Middlesbrough, was ruined for Tueart.
He missed City's triumphant second leg at Maine Road through
suspension.

Sending-off number three in the Tueart 'catalogue of crime'
came against yet another North-east club, this time minnows
Hartlepool in an F.A. Cup third round tie in January '76.

'I was sent-off with a bloke called George Potter, who I used
to go to college with! We did a business and administration course
together at Teesside Poly when I was at Sunderland.

'I slid in and he kicked me as I was getting up. So I nutted him
and we were both sent-off – only he had to go off on a stretcher!

'Generally, I wouldn't say I had a short temper. I was sent-off
a total of four times in my career. I just had a desire to win, to be

THE goal . . . Dennis makes contact to win the League Cup for City and claim one of the greatest ever Wembley goals.

best. Anyway that Hartlepool sending-off cost me an appearance against Boro, and I couldn't bear to watch the match.

'I went to a restaurant with my wife and a couple of friends and had the chef running back and forth with updates of the score. It was a disappointment to miss the semi, but the Final was the one I really wanted.'

Tueart's gravity-defying antics aside, the Final was a game that City fans will long remember for Doyle and Watson's superb handling of the Geordie's dangerous twin strikers Malcolm Macdonald and Alan Gowling.

'United had a good team, but Doyle was the man of the match for me,' says Dennis. 'He ended up marking Supermac most of the time and he did a brilliant job.'

In the aftermath of the triumph, Tueart was not alone in thinking the squad Tony Book had gathered – with the close season addition of prolific striker Brian Kidd – was about to go on to even greater things.

'But I had not appreciated just how much we would miss Colin Bell,' he says. 'We tried young Gary Owen and Paul Power there, bought Jimmy Conway from Fulham, but never ever replaced him.'

Nevertheless, City came within two points of winning the League title in 1976–77, inevitably losing out to Liverpool, although Tueart admits: 'It was never really that close.

'Liverpool had won it with two games to go and all we did was win our last two to make it look close. In reality, it was a five-point margin.'

That season also saw Tueart return to the European stage he had flirted with briefly in 1974 at Sunderland. And the UEFA Cup draw ensured Tueart tasted top-level action, with City facing Italian giants Juventus.

'That tie summed up our season really. We murdered them here but only won 1–0, and lost the return 2–0. We promised so much for that entire season but fell short.

'We were so close to really getting it right. It was the closest we had been for years to equalling United for average gates and Manchester was undoubtedly THE place to be. It was the nearest the city had been to recreating the Bell-Lee-Summerbee-Best-Law-Charlton years.'

Although Tueart was not to know it, the end of the '76–77 season also saw him win the last of his six England caps. In Belfast he was one of the scorers in a 2–1 win over Northern Ireland, but his international career ended on a disappointing note.

Successive Wembley defeats by Wales and Scotland – with Tueart making substitute appearances on both occasions – was hardly the stuff schoolboy football dreams are made of.

'I didn't do myself justice with England, although I don't think I was allowed to,' says Tueart. 'I seemed to sit on the bench every game because Don Revie didn't want to play with out and out wingers.

'When we failed to qualify for the '78 World Cup, I realised my chance had gone. I would have been in my thirties by the time it next came around. It was one of the reasons I eventually decided to go and play in the United States.

'I got six caps in three years and Colin Bell always said you need a dozen internationals to find your feet. And my caps came against Northern Ireland twice, Cyprus, Finland, Wales and Scotland – do you think they were trying to tell me something?!

'I'm proud to have represented my country, but it's not something I did with any success. I never got the chance to get my feet under the table, I always felt a spare part.'

Dissatisfaction with the path his international career was taking was just one of the contributory factors leading to Dennis

Celebrate! . . . a typical Tueart scene, celebrating his first goals for City on his return to Maine Road in March '80. He netted twice in a 2–2 draw with Bolton.

eventually leaving City early in 1978. The restless and ambitious streak in Tueart did not need much fuelling, and a series of events helped him decide his future lay away from Maine Road – 3,000 miles away.

'The side was hiccuping by this stage and I had some trouble with my hamstring,' he says. 'Peter Barnes was starting to mature, Tony was under pressure to play him more and more, and we had bought Mick Channon whose style just didn't fit in.'

Tueart's understandable frustration at a series of injuries spilled over as he watched another unsuccessful UEFA Cup venture from the unfamiliar position of the radio commentary booth.

A guest summariser on local radio, Tueart stormed down to the players' tunnel after a 2–2 draw with Widzew Lodz to 'express an opinion' to Ricky Kowenicki, the Polish defender involved in the sending-off of Willie Donachie, as Lodz stormed back from 2–0 down to grab a crucial draw.

The Tueart will-to-win apparently continued even from the sidelines, although the humour of the incident was probably lost on the commentator who found himself without his special guest on the final whistle.

However, it was a disagreement with Book over Tueart's best position that was the final straw for the fiery Geordie. He knew he had to leave Maine Road.

He explains: 'Even though I signed a fresh three-year contract in December '77, I went on the list at my own request and before long, an agent from the New York Cosmos contacted me to ask if I would be interested in playing over there.'

Tueart, still a current international, had understandably attracted domestic interest as well. Nottingham Forest assistant Peter Taylor desperately tried to get Tueart to sign for his and Brian Clough's thrilling Forest; QPR would have signed him at the drop of a hat. And then, there was Manchester United.

'I must be one of the few people to ever turn them down,' says Dennis with a grin. And, considering the bizarre circumstances of these particular negotiations, Tueart's smile is not misplaced.

'Peter Swales was very fair with me and promised he would tell me of any offers. At Christmas United came in and a meeting was set up with them at Tony Book's house in Sale.

'Dave Sexton was United's manager but I did most of the talking. To be honest he didn't excite me at all, though he talked of me replacing Gordon Hill and signing Gerry Francis.

'That night, I was playing pro-celebrity squash at Droylsden, standing in for John Cleese against the late Leonard Rossiter. Bill Taylor, our coach, was there and asked me about the meeting.

The volley . . . Tueart's calling card. This time he narrowly misses the mark for City in their fateful 4–0 League Cup win over Manchester United in 1975, the game in which Colin Bell was tragically injured.

'He told me to ask myself two things – whether the terms were better at United, and whether they had a better side.'

In both cases, decided Tueart, the answer was no and the phone call declining the Reds' offer was made from a pay phone at the squash club. To cap a memorable night, Tueart lost to Leonard Rossiter!

Instead, Tueart would head west for £235,000 to enjoy two successful and pioneering summers in the burgeoning North American Soccer League. But first, he left City fans with a tasty reminder of his ability. In 17 League appearances in the first half of '77–78, he hit the net 12 times – a run that included three hat-tricks.

Aston Villa, Chelsea and Newcastle (again) were on the receiving end of the Tueart magic. The final three-goal performance will long be remembered as the game in which Bell made his second emotional comeback from injury. But the hat-trick in City's impressive 4–1 win at Villa Park in the season's second game is the one that sticks in Tueart's mind.

'They were a good side and we were all looking forward to the game with it being at the start of the season,' he says. 'To me, that was a perfect stage and a powerful performance, not only by myself, but by the whole team.

'The first was an overhead kick – better than Wembley! – the second, I dispossessed somebody and slotted it past the keeper, and for the third I picked the ball up inside the halfway line, ran forward and lobbed Jimmy Rimmer.

'It just shows you what a strange game this is. We were flying and I thought we had a real chance of the title. Five months later I had left the club.'

Tueart's title premonitions were right. Only the title came Stateside. Inspired by Tueart – the first current England international to leave for the U.S.– Beckenbauer, Neeskens and Carlos Alberta, the Cosmos won the NASL Championship in '78, and were pipped by the Vancouver Whitecaps the following summer.

'I was 28 when I left, so I suppose the English game missed some of my best years, but it was worth it. For the financial rewards, the experience and the broadening of the mind, I would not have missed it.'

The American high life also provided Dennis with a vital grounding in the workings of big business. On his return after two years, he put his new-found knowledge to good use, laying the foundations of Premier Events, a company that would guarantee him a very secure future once his football days were over.

But that lay in the future. Tueart was still far from finished with City. The arrival of Brazilian Julio Mazzei as Cosmos' manager made Tueart and his European-style surplus to requirements.

With Derby County again leading the chase, Tueart decided it was time to come home. And that meant only one club.

'I found out City were interested but, with the dollar falling, Cosmos were trying to rip them off, asking more than they had paid for me. Malcolm Allison contacted me and talked about what he wanted to do.

'Eventually I said to him, "I know two Malcolm Allisons. The one Summerbee, Bell, Lee have told me about, and the one Channon, Hartford, Corrigan have told me about. The second one is no good to me, I need to know where I stand." '

Tueart's straight-talking worked. The move agreed, Tueart even told Allison how much to bid, then told New York, if they did not accept City's bid he would remain in the States for the final year of his contract.

Derby had unsuccessfully bid £250,000 for the player – he signed for City a second time in January 1980 for £150,000. Ever the budding entrepreneur, Tueart simply explains: 'I thought

A winner . . . Tueart, wearing the bottom half of the League Cup trophy after victory over Newcastle in 1976.

New York were taking advantage of the circumstances and I wasn't prepared to accept that for City, the club I had never really wanted to leave and which I now wanted to return to.'

City, of course, were a different proposition to the club Tueart had left behind. He returned to England just in time to hear of their demoralising F.A. Cup exit at lowly Halifax, and his five goals in 11 games were crucial in helping City stay up.

'I had left a squad with six current internationals and came back to find it full of babies. The place had been devastated,' he says. 'But I just got on with things; I wasn't influential in policy making decisions.'

Nevertheless, Tueart did have a hand – or, more accurately – a wrist to play when Allison finally parted company with the Blues in autumn 1980.

'I remember someone saying I helped end Malcolm's reign. We had lost 2–1 at Stoke and I got the goal but broke my wrist and missed three games in which we only got one point. Eventually, Malcolm was sacked after a loss at Leeds.

'Someone joked that if I had stayed in the side I might have snatched the odd goal and Malcolm might not have gone quite so soon.'

His replacement, John Bond, set City up for one of the most unbelievable turn-arounds in even this remarkable club's history. Having gone through the first dozen League games without a win, City stormed to the Centenary F.A. Cup Final, reached the semi-finals of the League Cup, and finished just below halfway in the first division.

Tueart, however, played in less than half the games.

'I have a lot of time for John Bond. Compared to Malcolm, he had a lot of sensible, good coaching ideas. Ultimately, his problem was that he was affected by being in the big time.

'He was playing me as a front man and we had a disagreement about my role. The good thing with Bondy was that he would let you have your say, and eventually we reached a compromise.

'I ended up playing in a midfield, attacking role, because John said my strength was playing facing goal. And I must admit, I felt very comfortable there.'

First, Tueart had a small role to play in the heartwrenching Cup Final replay loss to Spurs, coming on as a late substitute for Bobby McDonald. It was only his third appearance in City's cup run as his Maine Road career finally seemed to be reaching its conclusion.

'I remember standing on the pitch after the replay, watching Spurs go to collect the cup, and it was like there was no-one in the stadium apart from me. I was sure I was away and I said to myself, 'That's it. That's the blue shirt gone.'

'But Bond had other plans for Tueart. In his new midfield role alongside the re-signed Asa Hartford, and with Trevor Francis up front, Tueart starred in 15 of the first 18 League games in 1981–82, scoring an impressive nine goals.

'That was just about the best run of my life,' he says. 'But I snapped my achilles just before Christmas – funnily enough against Sunderland – and though I was back at the start of the next season and tried hard, it was never the same again.

'By then, I think the pressure of the Manchester scene was getting to Bondy and John Benson was appointed manager halfway through.'

Tueart's return, in the third game of the '82–83 relegation season was certainly unusual. Coming on as a substitute for injured goalkeeper Joe Corrigan, Tueart bagged the winner as City beat Watford 1–0 at Maine Road.

In typical City fashion, the last game of the 82–83 season provided a traumatic winner-take-all finale against a Luton Town side led by a tenacious midfield player later to become an important part of City history, called Brian Horton. A draw would preserve City's first division status; defeat and City would be a second division side for the first time in 17 years.

'My contract was up at the end of the season and I had spoken to the then chairman Peter Swales who said I would be alright for another year – but I knew that depended on us staying up,' says Dennis.

'Relegation would mean trimming the wage bill and, as the only first teamer whose contract was up, that would mean me going. So when the final whistle went and we had lost 1–0, no-one knew, apart from me and my wife, that my City career was over.

'The match couldn't be described as a game of football at all, it was dreadful—even the Luton goal was scrappy and deflected. Afterwards my emotions got the better of me. Brian, of all people, came up to me to shake my hand and I must admit we had a confrontation.

'I was really choked and it was just an expression of sadness. All this in front of 42,000 brilliant fans and with me knowing it was my last game; it was all so hard to swallow.'

Within days, the letter officially terminating Tueart's City career was delivered and he left for brief spells at Stoke City and Burnley as well as pursuing his fabulously successful career in the field of promotions and business development.

Finally, at the age of 34, Tueart announced to the Burnley team-mate with whom he shared a car to training that he was to retire when his contract ran out in the summer of 1984.

By a fitting coincidence, that training pal was Willie Donachie – the man whose cross had helped launch the Tueart legend at Wembley eight unforgettable years earlier.

Dennis Tueart
FULL INTERNATIONAL CAPS—6 (2 goals)

(England score given first)
1975: Cyprus (Limassol) sub 1–0, Northern Ireland (Belfast) 0–0
1976: Finland (Wembley) 2–1 GOAL.
1977: Northern Ireland (Belfast) 2–1 GOAL, Wales (Wembley)
       sub 0–1, Scotland (Wembley) sub 1–2.

MANCHESTER CITY APPEARANCES

League: 216 + 8 sub, 86 goals. F.A. Cup: 13, 3 goals. League Cup: 27, 18 goals. Europe: 3, 0 goals. TOTAL: 259 + 8 sub, 107 goals.

Manchester City
Honours

Football League: First Division Champions in 1936–37 and 1967–68; Runners-up in 1903–04, 1920–21 and 1976–77; Second Division Champions in 1989–99, 1902–03, 1909–10, 1927–28, 1946–47, 1965–66; Runners-up in 1895–6, 1950–51, 1988–89.

F.A. Cup: Winners in 1904, 1934, 1956, 1969; Runners-up in 1926, 1933, 1955 and 1981.

League Cup: Winners in 1970 and 1976; Runners-up in 1974.

F.A. Charity Shield: Winners in 1937, 1968 and 1972.

Full Members' Cup: Runners-up in 1986.

European competitions: European Cup Winners' Cup Winners in 1969–70; semi-finalists in 1970–71; Played in European Cup in 1968–69; Played in UEFA Cup in 1972–73, 1976–77, 1977–78 and 1978–79.